THE CAPE COD COOK BOOK

BY
SUZANNE CARY GRUVER

DOVER PUBLICATIONS, INC.
NEW YORK

Published in Canada by General Publishing Company, Ltd., 30 Lesmill Road, Don Mills, Toronto, Ontario.

Published in the United Kingdom by Constable and Company, Ltd., 10 Orange Street, London WC2H 7EG.

This Dover edition, first published in 1977, is an unabridged and unaltered republication of the work originally published by Little, Brown, and Company, Boston, in 1930.

International Standard Book Number: 0-486-23564-5
Library of Congress Catalog Card Number: 77-86263

Manufactured in the United States of America
Dover Publications, Inc.
180 Varick Street
New York, N.Y. 10014

FOREWORD

ONE way of having a good time has been to collect the recipes herewith presented, with the tang of the sea still on them. They are representative of both the old and the new Cape Cod. They have been gathered during many seasons of contact with Cape Cod folks, and from many sources: families of sea captains, famous for good living; managers of popular tea rooms dotting the Cape; the "lady who made that cake" at some notably good church supper (for happily they still carry on); and for several contributions, the sophisticated cooks of that floating population — the motoring and cottage-holding summer residents. The sophisticates are unmistakably "hard put to it" to hold their own with the native cooks. The ease with which a Cape Cod lady tosses up a juicy clam pie, or turns out a crockful of wafer-thin cookies is amazing, while her Aladdin-like construction of a four-storied layer cake is nothing short of an inspiration.

Some of the older recipes are family affairs and have not before appeared in print. The wording has frequently demanded revision. To "use judgment" in measurements was, once upon a time, a not unreasonable request, but ask it of a modern cook and you will speedily discover the extent of your presumption.

It has seemed well worth while to record as many of the good old dishes as were available. Sad are the prophecies anent the future of the New England kitchen. So let us enjoy the good things while we may, ere we return to the fruit-of-the-tree of our Darwinian ancestry or hasten on to the "efficiency" tabloid.

CONTENTS

Contents

THE CAPE COD COOK BOOK

EQUIVALENT WEIGHTS AND MEASURES

4 cups flour	= 1 pound
2 cups granulated sugar	= 1 pound
2½ cups powdered sugar	= 1 pound
10 eggs	= 1 pound
1 pint of liquid	= 1 pound
16 tablespoons	= 1 cup
3 teaspoons	= 1 tablespoon
4 tablespoons	= ¼ cup
2 tablespoons butter	= 1 ounce
1 teaspoon butter	= ⅙ ounce
Butter size of walnut	= ½ ounce
Butter size of an egg	= 2 ounces
1 cup butter	= ½ pound
1 cup white bread flour	= 4 ounces
1 teaspoonful	= 60 drops

Measurements used in recipes are for level cups or spoonfuls unless otherwise indicated. Use the back of a knife for leveling. Half spoonfuls are measured lengthwise of the spoon. Use a standard measuring cup, marked off in quarters, thirds, and halves.

QUANTITY SERVING

1 pound of coffee will make 50 cupfuls
8 pounds of fish will serve 12 or 14 people
1 pound of butter will serve 25
1 quart of soup will serve 4 or 5
5 quarts of lemonade will serve 25
1 gallon ice cream will serve 20
½ pint whipped cream makes 12 heaping tablespoons
5 pints boiled potatoes in salad makes 15 servings
A 12-pound ham will serve 20 or 25
A 15-pound roast will serve 25

BREAD CRUMBS

Dry all scraps of bread in a covered pan at the back of the stove. Run them through the meat grinder and sift. The coarser ones should be rolled and sifted again. Store them in fruit jars ready for immediate use. When a delicate color is important, the crumbs from freshly grated stale bread will be found better.

SOUPS AND CHOWDERS

FOUNDATION CREAM SOUP

3½ tablespoons butter   1 teaspoon salt
4 tablespoons flour   1 quart milk or milk and cream

Almost any vegetable pulp may be combined with this foundation to make a Cream Soup. The vegetable should be cooked, rubbed through a sieve, well seasoned, and the mixture beaten thoroughly after the cream is added.

Mix the ingredients like a white sauce, melting the butter, stirring in the flour and salt, and adding the milk gradually. Keep hot over a pan of boiling water while the vegetable pulp is being stirred in. Two cups of the pulp, or less, if strongly flavored, is a good proportion. If the pulp is very thick, mix the sauce with only half as much butter and flour as are given in the recipe.

CREAM OF ASPARAGUS SOUP

3 cups fresh asparagus, chopped   1½ tablespoons butter
3 cups water   1 teaspoon sugar
1½ tablespoons flour   3 cups milk
Salt, pepper

Simmer the asparagus in the water about half an hour, or until tender. Press hard through a sieve to obtain all the pulp possible. Save the water. Make a white sauce of the butter, flour, and seasonings. Combine with the asparagus pulp and water. Heat to boiling point but do not boil. A few choice tips may be reserved when pressing through the sieve, and added to the soup when serving. If canned asparagus is used, reserve all the tips and use the asparagus liquor in place of part of the water.

CREAM OF MUSHROOM SOUP

1 cup fresh mushrooms	1 quart milk
2 tablespoons butter	Salt, pepper
1 tablespoon flour	

Wash and drain the mushrooms. Cut them into pieces. Sauté in the butter six or eight minutes. Mix the flour with a portion of the milk and stir in. Blend well together. When smooth, add remainder of the milk. Simmer in double boiler half an hour. Add seasonings. Remove the finest of the mushrooms and press the others through a sieve, together with the soup. In serving, place the remainder of the mushrooms on top.

CREAM OF ONION SOUP

2½ cups sliced onions	1 quart milk or half milk and
2 tablespoons butter	half vegetable stock
2 tablespoons flour	1 egg yolk
	Salt, pepper

Fry the onions in the butter five minutes. Cover the dish and let simmer until soft, taking care not to brown them. Sprinkle with the flour and cook three minutes, while stirring. Add 3½ cups of the milk. Remove to double boiler. Cook half an hour. Rub through a sieve. Beat egg yolk slightly. Add it to remainder of milk and strain into the soup. Season and serve hot.

CREAM OF PEA SOUP

1 quart shelled peas	½ teaspoon sugar
2 cups boiling water or half stock, half water	1 tablespoon butter
	1 tablespoon flour
½ teaspoon salt	2 cups milk

Minced parsley, pepper

This is a good way of utilizing the older and harder garden peas. Boil the peas in the water or stock very slowly until tender. Set aside one cup of the peas. Mash the others with the water through a sieve.

Make a white sauce of the butter, flour, and milk, and stir into the soup. Add the seasonings, the reserved peas, and serve. Croutons are always acceptable with pea soup.

CREAM OF QUAHOG SOUP

30 quahogs or hard clams	1 teaspoon sugar
¼ cup clam juice	1 tablespoon butter
2 slices onion	1 tablespoon flour
1 quart milk	1 cup cream

Minced parsley

This delicious soup is a specialty of one of the smart Cape tea rooms.

Chop the quahogs very fine. Place them in a double boiler with the onion and clam juice. Cook without under dish for five minutes. Add milk and sugar. Place over hot water and let stand, but do not cook. Blend butter and flour and stir in. Cook three minutes. Strain and add cream. Serve in bouillon cups with a small round of toast covered with minced parsley on top.

CREAM OF SPINACH SOUP

2 cups cooked spinach	1 quart milk or half milk
1 teaspoon onion juice	and half vegetable stock
1 tablespoon butter	1 teaspoon celery salt
1 tablespoon flour	½ cup cream

If fresh spinach is used, wash thoroughly and boil fifteen minutes in salted water. Chop very fine. Press through a purée sieve. Blend butter and flour. Add to milk and place in double boiler with the spinach pulp. Cook over hot water twenty minutes, adding the seasonings toward the end. Add the cream, beat hard with an egg beater, and serve at once.

BAKED BEAN SOUP

3 cups cold baked beans	2 tablespoons flour
3 pints water	1½ cups stewed strained
2 slices onion	tomatoes
2 stalks celery	1 tablespoon chili sauce
2 tablespoons butter	Salt, pepper

Bring to a boil the beans, water, onion, and celery. Let simmer half an hour. Rub through a sieve. Add tomato and chili sauce. Cook together the butter and flour. Add salt and pepper. Combine mixtures and serve.

BLACK BEAN SOUP

2 cups black beans	1 hard-boiled egg
1 onion, sliced	½ teaspoon dry mustard
¼ cup celery, chopped	1 tablespoon butter
2 cloves	1 tablespoon flour
Brown stock or water	Salt, pepper

Soak the beans overnight. In the morning, drain. Add celery, onion, and cloves. Cover with fresh cold water. Boil slowly until the beans are tender. Rub all through a purée sieve. Add enough brown stock or water to make like thick cream. Mash the egg yolk with mustard and pepper and stir in. Cook butter and flour together until brown. Thin with a little stock and add to soup. Cook five minutes. Season. A spoonful of cooking sherry, which is now available, is an improvement. Serve with a slice of hard-boiled egg in each soup plate.

CORN CHOWDER

⅓ cup fat, salt pork, diced	Corn juice
1 small onion, sliced	1½ teaspoons salt
3 cups boiling water	¼ teaspoon celery salt
3 cups potatoes, diced	2 cups hot milk
1 can corn, chopped	4 or 6 Boston crackers, split

Try out the pork. Cook onion in the fat ten minutes. Add boiling water and strain into soup kettle. Add potatoes and salt. Cook fifteen minutes or until tender. Strain corn juice into kettle. Add chopped corn, hot milk, and crackers. Cook five minutes more.

CHICKEN BROTH

Remainder of cooked chicken	2 teaspoons salt
1½ quarts water	2 teaspoons rice

Remove all the pieces of meat and place with the broken bones in a soup kettle with the cold water and salt. Simmer four or five hours, now and then skimming off the fat that rises to the surface. Strain. Place the strained liquor with the washed rice in a saucepan and simmer until the rice is tender.

CLAM BISQUE

2 cups clams, chopped	1 quart soup stock or half
Clam liquor	stock, half water
½ cup uncooked rice	1 cup cream
A stalk of celery, salt, and a sprig of parsley	

Cook the clams in their own liquor and chop very fine. Place in a kettle with the stock, rice, and seasonings. Boil until the rice is tender. Strain through a sieve, pressing through as much of the rice and clams as possible. Strain a second time and reheat. Add the cream and beat all together with an egg beater just before serving.

CLAM BROTH

½ peck clams   Whipped cream
1 cup cold water

Scrub clams thoroughly, using several rinsing waters. When free from sand, place in a kettle with a lid. Add the water and steam until shells open. Strain the liquid through a cheesecloth and serve hot in cups with a spoonful of whipped cream on top.

CLAM CHOWDER

1 quart of clams, solid	1 onion, sliced
Clam juice	3 level tablespoons butter
1 slice fat, salt pork	3 level tablespoons flour
2 cups potatoes, pared and diced	3 cups scalded milk
	1 teaspoon salt

⅛ teaspoon pepper

Pour two cups of cold water over the clams to cleanse. Double a piece of cheesecloth and strain both water and clam juice through. Chop hard portions of clams. Cut the pork into bits and try out. Cook the onion in the fat until yellowed and soft but not dark colored. Add water and strained clam juice. Let simmer ten minutes. Parboil the potatoes five minutes. Rinse in cold water and drain. Strain the onion water and drippings over the potatoes. Add the chopped clams. Cook all together until potatoes are tender. Then add soft parts of the clams and cook three minutes more.

Mix the blended butter and flour with the milk and stir in.   Combine all.   Season to taste and serve.

CLAM AND MUSHROOM SOUP

2 quarts clams, in shells	3 tablespoons flour
1 pound fresh mushrooms	1 cup cream
3 tablespoons butter	Salt, pepper

Steam the clams to obtain the liquor.   If there are not three pints, add water to make that amount. Clean the mushrooms.   Chop the stems and trimmings to use in the soup, reserving the best of the mushrooms to use otherwise.   Simmer trimmings for an hour in the clam broth.   Brown the butter, blend in the flour.   Strain the stock through a cheesecloth.   Add flour and butter gradually.   Simmer ten minutes more.   Add seasonings and the cream, and serve.

EMERGENCY SOUP

1 small can salmon	2 tablespoons flour
1 quart milk, either fresh	1 teaspoon salt
or evaporated diluted	1 teaspoon celery salt
1 tablespoon butter	White pepper

This is unusually good for a quickly prepared soup which must be made from materials at hand.

Remove the skin and bits of bones from the fish. Scald the milk.   Thicken with butter and flour

blended. Season. Add the fish and boil up once.
A tablespoon of minced parsley adds flavor.

FISH CHOWDER — "DANIEL WEBSTER"

This, in his own words, is Daniel Webster's recipe
for Fish Chowder. "Suitable," he said, "for a
large fishing party."

"Take a cod of ten pounds, well cleaned, leaving
on the skin. Cut into pieces one and a half pounds
thick, preserving the head whole. Take one and a
half pounds of clear, fat, salt pork, cut in thin slices.
Do the same with twelve potatoes. Take the largest
pot you have. Try out the pork first; then take
out the pieces of pork, leaving in the drippings.
Add to that three parts of water, a layer of fish, so
as to cover the bottom of the pot; next, a layer of
potatoes, then two tablespoons of salt, 1 teaspoon of
pepper, then the pork, another layer of fish, and the
remainder of the potatoes.

" Fill the pot with water to cover the ingredients.
Put it over a good fire, let the chowder boil twenty-
five minutes. When this is done, have a quart of
boiling milk ready, and ten hard crackers split
and dipped in cold water. Add milk and crackers.
Let the whole boil five minutes. The chowder is
then ready and will be first-rate if you have followed
the directions. An onion may be added if you like
the flavor."

FISH CHOWDER — "PROVINCETOWN"

4 pounds fresh cod or haddock	2 tablespoons butter
4 medium-sized potatoes	2 tablespoons flour
2 slices fat, salt pork	2 cups milk
1 onion	Salt, pepper

Boston crackers

Discard skin and bones, and cut the fish into small chunks. Pare and slice the potatoes, covering them with water until needed. Slice the fat pork and try out in frying pan. Slice the onion and fry in the fat. In a chowder kettle, place a layer of fish. Season with salt and pepper. Add a layer of potatoes, then the onion and drippings, and so on until all is used. Cover with three cups of cold water — or more if necessary. Simmer until potatoes are soft. Blend the butter, flour, and milk, and stir in. Season to taste. Add crackers and serve.

LOBSTER BISQUE — "WESTLOOK"

1 small lobster	4 tablespoons butter
1 quart milk	6 tablespoons flour

Celery salt, paprika

Remove meat from the lobster and dice. Break up the shell, claws included. Cover shell with cold water and simmer an hour or more. Then strain off the liquid and heat in double boiler with the milk. In a small pan, melt the butter, stir in the flour, and cook two minutes, then add to the hot liquid. Whisk and stir until smooth and thickened. Put in the diced lobster meat and seasonings, adding cream or butter if a richer bisque is desired. Serve in bouillon cups. If the lobster has the coral, wash it and force through a fine strainer. Cream it with a teaspoon of butter and add a teaspoon of flour. When well mixed, stir into the soup. This gives added color and richness.

ONION SOUP WITH CHEESE

7 medium-sized onions	Grated cheese
3 tablespoons butter	Kitchen Bouquet, salt,
5 cups stock or warm water	pepper
Rounds of rye bread	

Melt the butter and cook the nicely sliced onions until quite brown but very slowly — allowing fifteen minutes for this. When quite soft, scrape with the fat into a covered kettle, adding remaining butter, salt, pepper, and the stock or warm water. Let cook slowly half an hour, keeping kettle closely covered. Stir in a teaspoon of bottled Kitchen Bouquet for coloring and added flavor. Place a round of rye bread in the middle of each soup plate. Cover it thickly with grated cheese and pour the hot soup around.

ONION AND BEAN CHOWDER

2 cups minced onions	5 potatoes
½ cup butter or fat	4 cups hot milk
1 cup baked beans	Salt, pepper

The early Cape Cod chowder was in itself a substantial meal. One of the most primitive of dishes, the recipes are being sought out and presented to modern households as "Combination" dishes. Chicken fat was invariably used instead of butter.

Cook, but do not brown, the onions in the hot fat in covered pan until soft — about half an hour. Add the potatoes pared and sliced, and the beans. Minced parsley or other herbs put into the kettle add flavor. Cook until the potatoes are tender. Serve very hot.

OLD-FASHIONED PARSNIP CHOWDER

2 cups chopped parsnips	1 quart milk
1 cup potatoes, diced	2 cups boiling water
⅓ cup fat salt pork	4 tablespoons fat or butter
4 slices onions	½ cup rolled cracker crumbs

Salt, pepper, parsley

Pare parsnips and potatoes and cut into cubes. Cut up the salt pork and try out. Add onion and cook five minutes. Remove scraps. Put in parsnips and potatoes, a few at a time. Sprinkle with salt and pepper. Place in chowder kettle, add boiling water, and cook until vegetables are soft. Then add the crumbs, milk, butter, and minced parsley.

OYSTER STEW

1 pint or 3 cups oysters	2 tablespoons butter
1 quart milk	1½ teaspoons salt

Paprika

Look over the oysters carefully to remove bits of shell. Then cook in their own liquor until edges curl. Remove scum that rises. Scald the milk but do not allow it to boil. Add butter, seasonings, oysters, and oyster liquor.

SALT CODFISH CHOWDER

1½ pounds salt codfish	2 onions, sliced
1 quart potatoes, pared and sliced	Hot milk to cover
	2 tablespoons butter

Shred the fish. Soak in hot water an hour or more. Drain. Soak once more. Prepare the potatoes. Place a layer in chowder kettle. Then a layer of fish, onion, pepper and salt if needed. Cover all with hot milk, and simmer slowly until potatoes and fish are soft. Add butter just before dishing up.

SCOTCH BROTH

1 pound mutton from neck or leg	1 tablespoon minced parsley
4 tablespoons pearl barley	1½ tablespoons butter
2 tablespoons each of diced carrots, onion, turnip, and celery	½ tablespoon flour
	1 tablespoon salt
	Pepper

Pour boiling water over the barley and let soak overnight. Remove meat from mutton bones, discarding skin and fat. Put bones covered with water on fire and simmer. Cut meat into cubes and boil quickly, skimming water while cooking. Add remaining ingredients, together with water from the bones, and cook slowly until barley is soft.

TOMATO BISQUE

2 cups stewed tomatoes	1 tablespoon flour
1 teaspoon minced onion	1 quart milk, scalded
1 tablespoon butter	Whipped cream
¼ teaspoon soda	1 teaspoon sugar

Salt, paprika

Heat the tomatoes, onion, and butter for fifteen minutes. Sift soda and stir in. Thicken with the flour blended with a little cold milk. Add slowly to scalded milk, and season. Strain.

If served in cups, a spoonful of whipped cream is a desirable addition.

TOMATO CHOWDER

1 quart tomatoes, canned or fresh	3 tablespoons pork cubes
¼ cup rice	1 quart boiling water
2 onions, chopped	1 tablespoon flour
	2 teaspoons salt

Boston crackers

If tomatoes are fresh, they must be stewed until soft. Try out the pork. Cook the onions in the fat until soft, but light brown. Scrape into a kettle. Add the rice, tomatoes, and water. Cover tight and cook slowly about one hour, or until rice is tender. Thicken with the flour mixed to a paste with water. Add seasonings to taste. Place split crackers in the tureen and pour the hot chowder over.

VEGETABLE CHOWDER — "PROVINCETOWN"

½ cup fat salt pork bits, or
4 tablespoons drippings
1 cup potatoes, peeled and
   diced
1 cup carrots, diced

1 cup turnips, diced
1 onion, sliced
2 cups hot milk
3 tablespoons flour
Celery salt, pepper

Try out the pork scraps or melt drippings. Remove scraps and pour the fat into a chowder kettle with all the vegetables, seasonings, and water to cover. Cook until vegetables are tender. Add milk. Let come to boiling point and thicken with flour, thinned with a little cold water. Do not boil after milk is added, but merely reach that point and keep very hot.

FISH

FISH NOTES

When boiling fish, a tablespoon of vinegar in the water will preserve the whiteness. The water should just cover the fish.

BROTH FOR BOILING FISH

2 quarts of water	2 sliced carrots
2 tablespoons vinegar	4 cloves
2 sliced onions	2 sprigs of parsley
2 tablespoons salt	1 or 2 bay leaves
3 stalks diced celery	

Boil all ingredients together before using as a liquid in which to boil the fish. This is sometimes called a Court Bouillon. It gives a most delicious flavor to what would otherwise be a flat-tasting boiled fish. Strain and use.

The extra quantity may be strained through a cheesecloth and bottled for future use.

To Boil Fish

Cover the prepared fish with the hot broth and simmer very gently until the flesh begins to separate from the bones. Never boil fish hard. Allow six to ten minutes for each pound for boiling, depending on the thickness of the fish. A large fish should be cut into fillets of a size for serving before boiling.

To Test Fresh Fish

If fish is fresh, the eyes will be bright and bulging. The flesh, when pressed with the finger, will be elastic. The gills — the fringelike appendage each side of the head — will be bright red. Fresh fish, if dropped into water, will sink. If the fish floats, it is unfit for use.

To Freshen Salt Fish

Cover the fish with water and let stand, flesh side down, overnight. Drain and cover with fresh water in the morning, if the fish is still salty. Place the fish on a rack a little above the bottom of the dish and the salt will more readily drop away. Discard this salt and water. If the fish is to be boiled in broth, it does not require so long soaking.

BAKED BLUEFISH — "GREY GABLES"

1 Buzzards Bay bluefish	2 cups bread crumbs
3 or 4 slices fat salt pork	¾ teaspoon mixed poultry
2 tablespoons melted butter	dressing, or sage
1 tablespoon minced onion	Salt, pepper

Have the fish freshly caught, cleaned, and prepared for baking. Wipe with wet cloth. Dry well. Rub inside and out with salt and pepper mixed. Make a fish stuffing of crumbs, butter, onion, and season-

ings, adding water to make pliable, but not wet.
Stuff fish and sew up.   Lay several slices of salt pork
in a greased and heated baking pan.   Put in the fish.
Dredge with flour, salt and pepper.   Bake in moderately hot oven, allowing fifteen minutes to each
pound of fish.   Baste with drippings in pan.

BROILED BLUEFISH — "JEFFERSON"

Have the fish split and prepared for broiling.
Dust surfaces with salt and pepper.   Brush over with
oil or melted butter.   If cooked in gas oven, place
skin side down, under the flame, reducing heat when
nearly done.   Cook until nicely browned.   Do not
turn fish over, as the flesh side alone requires direct
heat.   Serve with new potatoes and Maître d'Hôtel
Butter.   (See "Fish Sauces.")

BROOK TROUT — "SPORTSMAN"

An expert angler gives his recipe for cooking
trout.   "Remove the fins but not the tails or heads.
Do not flour them.   Simply salt a very little.   Mix
bacon fat and butter in the pan.   When very hot
put in the trout, after drying them thoroughly.
Turn over only once.   Lemon slices do not belong
with trout.   The acid spoils the delicate flavor.
And watercress is a more suitable accompaniment
than parsley."

BAKED STUFFED COD

Codfish, the insignia of Massachusetts, is sometimes referred to as "The Cape Cod Turkey." To serve it, baked and stuffed, follow instructions for "Baked Bluefish", using the same stuffing or the one given under "Fish Stuffing." As cod is inclined to dryness, place a few small slices of the fat pork across the back after sewing up and arranging in the pan. Tomato or Horseradish Sauce may be passed with it.

CODFISH CAKES WITH BACON

3 medium-sized potatoes	1 egg
½ box shredded codfish	Strips of bacon
Butter size of large egg	Pepper

The fish cakes are best when mixed the night before and allowed to stand until time to fry them for breakfast. Boil white potatoes until soft. Moisten codfish in cold water. Drain well. Add butter and pepper to taste, then the egg, and beat all together until very light and fluffy. This mixture should stand overnight, covered. Fry bacon strips for each person for breakfast. When crisp, remove bacon, and keep fat hot. Mold the fish mixture very lightly into cakes and fry on both sides in the hot fat.

CODFISH BALLS — "PROVINCETOWN"

1 cup dried codfish	1 round tablespoon butter
2 cups potatoes	1 egg
Salt, pepper	

Soak the fish several hours until softened. Boil the potatoes and beat up with the butter until light and smooth. A fork is best for this. Pick out all the bones from the fish. Break it into small pieces and add to the potatoes. Beat the egg well and add. Season with salt and pepper. Beat again with the fork. Flour the hands and roll the mixture into tiny balls. Drop these, a few at a time, into deep, hot fat for one minute, or just long enough to brown.

CREAMED CODFISH

1 cup dried codfish	1 tablespoon flour
1 tablespoon butter	1 cup hot milk

Pepper

Freshen the fish by soaking several hours. Pick it into small pieces. Make a sauce of the butter, flour, and hot milk. Add the fish and beat well.

A beaten egg stirred into the sauce makes it richer. Serve with boiled or mashed potatoes. For seasoning, a little pepper is usually liked, but the salt depends upon the freshness of the fish.

SCALLOPED COD WITH CHEESE

2 pounds fresh cod	1 cup hot milk
2 tablespoons butter	Bread crumbs, buttered
2 tablespoons flour	2 tablespoons grated cheese

Salt, pepper

Boil the fish in salted water until tender. Drain. Separate it into flakes. Cook butter and flour together until bubbling and add slowly to the hot milk. Cook until creamy. Season with salt and pepper. Butter a baking dish. Place a layer of crumbs at the bottom, then a layer of fish flakes. Spread with a portion of the white sauce. Repeat. Cover the top with grated cheese and buttered crumbs. Bake half an hour in a moderate oven.

CODFISH SOUFFLÉ

1 cup shredded codfish	2 eggs
2 cups mashed potatoes	2 cups milk
Salt, pepper	

Moisten the codfish with hot water. Mix with the other ingredients and beat hard together. Season to taste. Butter a dish just large enough to hold the mixture, and bake three-quarters of an hour in moderate oven or at 350° F.

COD TONGUES

As these are usually salted, they must be soaked overnight. Drain. Boil ten minutes in fresh water. Serve with a good butter sauce. If preferred fried, wash them well to remove salt, dip into flour, and fry in butter.

CLAM CAKES — "EAST SANDWICH"

1 pint clams, freed from shells	2 teaspoons baking powder
	2 eggs, slightly beaten
1 pint flour	Milk to mix

Chop the clams or run through a grinder. Make a batter of flour, baking powder, eggs, and milk, using just enough milk to let the batter drop easily from a spoon. Beat well together and stir in the clams. Grease a frying pan with bacon or pork fat. Drop in the mixture by spoonfuls. Fry brown on both sides. Scallops, cut into halves and parboiled, are also very nice prepared in this way.

CLAM COCKTAILS

Little Neck clams are best for cocktails. Chill them well before using. Serve five in each small glass, cover with Cocktail Mixture (See "Fish and Meat Sauces"), and set the glasses in cracked ice when serving.

FRIED CLAMS

Follow the recipe given for Fried Oysters.

CLAM FRITTERS

Prepare a mixture as for Clam Cakes. Drop from a spoon into deep, hot fat. When light brown, remove and drain on paper.

CLAM OMELET

5 or 6 hard clams	½ cup milk
1 tablespoon butter	3 eggs
1 tablespoon flour	Salt, pepper

Chop the clams fine. Make a white sauce of the butter, flour, salt, and milk. Separate the eggs. Beat the yolks until creamy. Mix with the white sauce. Add the clams. Beat the whites stiff and fold in. Heat the butter in an omelet pan and turn in the mixture. Cook slowly until it has risen. When brown on the bottom, place in a hot oven to cook on top. Crease, fold over, and serve.

CLAM PIE OR SEA CLAM PIE

2 cups hard clams
4 common or Boston crackers, rolled
1 egg
1 cup milk
1 tablespoon melted butter
¾ teaspoon poultry seasoning or thyme
Salt, pepper

Chop the clams, or run them, with the crackers, through a food chopper. Beat the egg slightly. Combine the ingredients. Bake between two rich pie crusts in a deep plate.

CLAMS SCALLOPED WITH MACARONI

½ pound macaroni
1 tablespoon butter
1 teaspoon minced onion
1 tablespoon flour
Salt, pepper
2 cups clams, drained and chopped
Clam juice
½ cup grated cheese
Boiling water

Cook the macaroni in salted boiling water until tender. Melt the butter and fry the onion, but do not brown. Blend in the flour and add the milk

gradually. Heat the drained clam juice in half a
cup of boiling water and stir in slowly. Beat all
together as it thickens. Butter a baking dish and
arrange alternate layers of macaroni and clams.
Add seasoning to the hot sauce and pour over all.
Sprinkle the grated cheese on top. Bake about
twenty-five minutes or until lightly browned.

CLAM SOUFFLÉ

1 cup clams, minced	1 cup milk
1 cup clam juice	1 tablespoon lemon juice
4 tablespoons butter	2 egg whites
or substitute	1 cup fine bread crumbs
5 tablespoons flour	Salt, pepper

Heat the clam juice and milk in a double boiler.
Melt the butter and blend in the flour until bubbling,
then mix with the heated milk and clam juice to
make a smooth sauce. Sprinkle lemon juice over the
clams and let stand. Remove sauce from fire. Add
clams and seasonings. Beat egg whites stiff and
fold in. Butter a small mold or ramekins. Fill
two thirds full with the mixture. Cover the top
with the crumbs mixed with melted butter. Bake
about ten minutes in hot oven or at 425° F.

STEAMED CLAMS — "WESTLOOK"

Clams in the shell, freshly dug	2 onions, sliced
	½ teaspoon white pepper
Melted butter	

Wash and scrub the clams thoroughly to remove all sand. Heat a kettle. Put in the clams. Sprinkle over them the sliced onions and the pepper. Cover and steam twenty minutes. Take from the kettle and serve piping hot with individual dishes of melted butter. Strain the broth from the kettle and serve in cups. The flavor will be found delicious.

DEVILED CRABS

2 cups crab meat
1 tablespoon butter
1 tablespoon flour
1 cup rich milk
2 eggs well beaten
Grated onion
Salt, pepper
Crab shells

Cook the butter, flour, and milk until thick and creamy. Add the seasonings, crab meat, and beaten eggs. Place over hot water. Stir until thickened, then remove from fire. When somewhat cooled, fill crab shells, sprinkle on fine bread crumbs, brush over with oil or melted butter, and brown in the oven.

EMERGENCY FISH PIE

1 medium-sized can tuna fish
1 teaspoon lemon juice
2 tablespoons butter
2 tablespoons flour
1 cup milk
Pie paste
½ cup boiled onions, cut up
¼ cup cooked carrots, diced
¾ cup cooked peas
1 hard-boiled egg, sliced
Salt, pepper, nutmeg

Flake the fish, discarding the skin and all dark bits. Sprinkle with lemon juice and let stand. Make a white sauce of the butter, flour, and milk. Mix with the fish and add seasonings. Line a deep baking dish with thin pastry. Fill with alternate layers of the creamed fish and the vegetables. Cover the top with a slit crust and bake brown in a hot oven or at 425° F.

FLAKED FISH, WITH CHEESE SAUCE

2 cups cooked fish	1 cup milk
2 tablespoons butter	¾ cup grated cheese
2 tablespoons flour	Salt, pepper

Almost any kind of fish may be used, but halibut, cod, and salmon are especially good.

Make a cheese sauce by blending the melted butter with the flour, adding the milk gradually and the cheese stirred in last. Cook together over hot water until the cheese has melted. Season well and mix with the fish. Place in a buttered baking dish. Mashed potato piped around the edge of the dish with a pastry tube makes a pretty garnish. Brown in a hot oven.

CURRIED FISH, WITH RICE TIMBALES

2 cups boiled rice	1 teaspoon lemon juice
2 cups flaked boiled fish, fresh or canned	2 teaspoons curry powder
3 tablespoons butter or oil	1 cup milk, heated
4 tablespoons flour	1 cup fish stock or equivalent

Prepare the timbales first. Wet small timbale molds, or a large ring mold, inside. Pack in the rice thoroughly. Let stand in a pan of hot water to keep hot.

Prepare the fish, removing all bits of skin or bone. Cover with the lemon juice. Make a sauce of the melted butter, flour, curry powder, stock, and hot milk. Season with salt and pepper and add the fish, stirring in a little extra butter or cream to make a smooth mixture.

Invert the large timbale, if used, on a hot platter and place the curried fish in the middle. If the small timbales are used, place them at intervals around the edge of a platter and garnish with slices of hard-boiled eggs and parsley sprigs.

PLANKED FISH

Bluefish, shad, mackerel, halibut, and cod, are all excellent for planked cooking. Clean and dry the fish. Prepare the plank by oiling and heating it in a hot oven. Marinate the fish in a little oil with two slices of onion and the juice of half a lemon. Brush the surface of the fish with the oil and arrange on the plank when it is hot. Put into a moderate oven or at 375° F. A thin fish will be cooked in twelve or fifteen minutes, but a thick fish will need a half hour's cooking. Fill a pastry bag with mashed potato. Five minutes before the fish is done, take it from the oven and pipe a border of rosettes around the edge of the plank, leaving a space between the

potato and the fish for other vegetables. Brush the
rosettes with beaten egg yolk. Return to the oven
to brown. Prepare several kinds of hot cooked
vegetables — carrots, spinach, cauliflower — and
place in mounds around the plank. Spread the hot
fish with butter, minced parsley, and lemon juice
and serve.

FILLETS OF FLOUNDER

These are good either fried or baked. When fried,
they are sometimes presented in restaurants as sole,
a favorite French fish not found in American waters.
Prepare them by marinating in oil and lemon juice.
Roll in flour, beaten egg, and fine bread crumbs, and
fry in oil or butter until delicately browned.

FILLETS OF BAKED FLOUNDER

¾ can mushrooms	1 slice onion
1 cup fish stock or	1 tablespoon cooking sherry
mushroom liquor	Salt, pepper, fine bread crumbs
Parsley or celery stalk	

Chop the mushrooms with the onion and a sprig
of parsley or celery stalk. Sprinkle on the sherry
and mix with the stock. Butter a shallow baking
dish. Place a portion of the mixture on the bottom.
Lay the fillets on this. Salt and pepper lightly and
pour the remainder of the sauce over them. Cover
with fine crumbs and bits of butter. Bake about

Fish

33

forty minutes or until the fish is tender. Sauté remainder of the mushrooms in melted butter and garnish edges of the platter. Keep the fish moist while baking, using cream if needed.

HADDOCK À LA RAREBIT

1 cup milk	2 cups cheese, cut fine
Butter size of an egg	1 teaspoon dry mustard
2 tablespoons flour	Salt, pepper

Have the haddock split and the bone removed. Make a sauce of the butter, flour, and milk, adding the seasonings and cheese last. Place the fish in a buttered earthenware dish which can be sent to table. Pour the sauce over it and bake half an hour or until tender and lightly browned.

HALIBUT BAKED WITH CHEESE

2 tablespoons butter	Salt, paprika
2 tablespoons flour	2 cups grated cheese
2 cups milk	

Prepare slices of halibut cut three-quarters of an inch thick. Make a white sauce of the butter, flour, milk, and seasonings. Stir in the grated cheese, which should be of a soft variety like American. Place the halibut slices in a buttered baking dish and pour the sauce over and around them. Bake until the fish is tender.

HALIBUT BAKED WITH TOMATO SAUCE

2 pounds halibut	1 cup stock or water
2 cups fresh tomatoes	3 tablespoons butter
1 slice onion	3 tablespoons flour

1 teaspoon sugar

Cook together the tomatoes, onion, sugar, and stock or water for twenty minutes. Blend the butter and flour, cook until bubbling, then stir into the tomatoes. Cook until thickened. Strain. Place the fish in a buttered baking pan. Pour half the sauce around it. Bake thirty-five minutes, basting from time to time. When the fish is served, pour the remainder of the sauce around the platter.

BOILED HALIBUT, WITH EGG SAUCE

2 or more pounds of fish cut for boiling	1½ tablespoons flour
	1 cup hot milk
2 tablespoons melted butter	2 hard-boiled eggs

To boil fish, see "Broth" under "Fish Notes." If limited for time, prepare boiling water with one tablespoon vinegar and one teaspoon salt to each quart of water. Tie the fish in a cheesecloth to facilitate handling. Simmer gently, allowing ten minutes to each pound. It is cooked when the flesh begins to separate from the bones.

Make a sauce of the butter, flour, and milk. When well blended, add the seasonings, and the eggs cut into slices.

HALIBUT TIMBALES, WITH LOBSTER SAUCE

2 cups boiled halibut
2 teaspoons lemon juice
½ teaspoon onion juice

1 teaspoon Worcestershire Sauce
1 egg, separated
2 cups thick white sauce

Mince the halibut fine. Mix with the seasonings
and the white sauce. Beat the egg yolk slightly and
mix in. Fold in the stiffly beaten egg white. Place
rounds of greased white paper in the bottom of small
timbale molds. Oil the sides of the molds. Pour in
the mixture. Bake in a pan of hot water about
twenty-five minutes. After removing from oven, let
stand awhile in a warm place, before turning out on a
warm platter or individual plates. Pour the Lobster
Sauce around the timbales. Tomato or Parsley Sauce
are also good.   (See under "Fish and Meat Sauces.")

BAKED STUFFED LOBSTER — "THERMIDOR"

1 freshly boiled lobster
2 tablespoons butter
1 teaspoon shallots or
  young onions

½ cup thin white sauce
½ tablespoon "made" mustard
2 tablespoons cooking sherry
2 egg yolks
1 tablespoon cream

Split the lobster into halves. Remove meat.
Wash shell. Melt butter in a saucepan. Sauté
the lobster meat a few minutes until well heated
through. Mix together the white sauce, shallots,
mustard, and sherry. Add to the lobster and
simmer gently two minutes. Remove from fire.
Beat in the egg yolks and cream. Mix all well

together and fill the halves of the lobster shell. Set into a hot oven to bake until browned.

BROILED LIVE LOBSTER

The lobster loses nothing in flavor and is far more easily handled by being boiled a short time before being split in two down the back. Discard the stomach and intestines. Remove the coral and green substance, which is the liver. Spread upon an oiled broiler and rub over with melted butter or oil. Have the shell side toward the flame for about fifteen minutes, then turn the flesh side, and cook five minutes. Lift broiler from time to time to prevent scorching. Melt half a cup of butter and stir in the liver. Mince the coral and use with the butter as a sauce poured over the lobster when serving.

BUTTERED LOBSTER

1 pound lobster meat   3 tablespoons butter
Salt, pepper, lemon juice

Chop the meat coarsely. Melt butter and sauté the lobster meat until heated thoroughly. Season with lemon juice, pepper or paprika, and salt. Serve very hot on thin slices of toast.

LOBSTER COCKTAIL

Cold boiled lobster meat   1 teaspoon lemon juice
2 tablespoons chili sauce   1 tablespoon cooking sherry
1 tablespoon tomato catsup   Onion juice, paprika

Cut the lobster into inch pieces and set away to chill. When ready to serve, place five or six pieces in each small cocktail glass and cover with the sauce, made by mixing together the ingredients as given. Cooking sherry now available has enough salt in it so that little if any extra salt is necessary.

LOBSTER CROQUETTES

1½ cups lobster meat, minced
5 tablespoons oil or butter
6 tablespoons flour
1½ cups milk, heated
½ teaspoon salt
1 tablespoon lemon juice
Bread or cracker crumbs
1 egg, beaten
2 tablespoons cold water

Heat the butter or oil and blend in the flour. Add hot milk to make a smooth mixture. When thick and creamy, add the seasonings and lobster. Spread out on a flat dish to cool. Dilute the beaten egg with water. Roll the crumbs fine and sift them. Shape the croquettes, roll in crumbs, egg, and crumbs again. Mold them several hours in advance and set away to dry. Fry in deep hot fat.

Serve with Anchovy or Tartare Sauce.

LOBSTER NEWBURG — "MONUMENT BEACH"

2 cups fresh lobster meat
3 egg yolks
2 tablespoons cooking sherry
Juice of ¼ lemon
3 tablespoons butter
1 cup cream
Paprika, nutmeg

Cut the lobster into small even pieces. Sprinkle over it half the sherry and the lemon juice. Let stand half an hour in a cool place.

When ready to serve, melt the butter and put in the lobster meat. Cook, closely covered, for six minutes, or until thoroughly heated. Pour on the remainder of the sherry and cover again for a few minutes. Heat the cream over hot water. Beat egg yolks slightly and stir in. When it begins to thicken, remove and add very slowly to the lobster. Do not allow to boil or it will curdle. Remove from fire as soon as well combined. Sprinkle on a little paprika and grated nutmeg. Serve immediately. Salt is not usually needed with the present cooking sherry.

BAKED FRESH MACKEREL

An excellent way of cooking a nice fresh mackerel is to have the fish split for broiling. Then place it skin side down on a well-oiled paper in a baking pan. Sprinkle pepper, bits of butter, and minced parsley over the fish. Cover the bottom of the pan with milk. Set into a hot oven to bake. When the milk is absorbed, the fish will be tender and nicely browned. The paper facilitates removal from the pan.

BROILED SALT MACKEREL

Soak the fish overnight. Drain. Cover with boiling water one hour. Rinse in cold water. Dry thoroughly. Brush surfaces with salad oil mixed with lemon juice or vinegar and let stand to absorb. Split the fish and place on an oiled broiler. Broil the skin side about seven minutes, and the flesh side twice as long, unless the fish is very thin, when less time will be required. Serve with Maître d'Hôtel Butter. (See "Sauces.")

BOILED SALT MACKEREL

Soak the fish and drain as in above recipe. When ready to cook, simmer fifteen minutes in "Broth for Boiling Fish" (See "Fish Notes"), or add to the boiling water one teaspoon vinegar, one slice onion, a bay leaf or sprig of parsley. Serve with small boiled potatoes and Parsley Butter. A good egg sauce is always liked with this fish.

OYSTER COCKTAILS

Allow five small chilled oysters (Cotuits are very good) for each cocktail.

Place them in a glass and pour over enough of the Cocktail Mixture (see "Fish and Meat Sauces") to cover. The glasses should be set in cracked ice when serving.

CREAMED OYSTERS

Clean the oysters and look over carefully for bits of shell. Simmer in their own juice until plump.

Do not allow them to boil.   If they are to be served on toast, make a thin white sauce, using a portion of the oyster juice in place of all milk.   Put the oysters into the sauce and set the pan over hot water to reheat.   If the oysters are to be used as a filling for patty shells, make a thick white sauce.   Season with celery salt and a little onion juice.   Stir in a beaten egg at the last to make a richer sauce.

ESCALLOPED OYSTERS

1 pint oysters	½ cup milk
1 cup cracker crumbs	Oyster juice, strained
Butter, salt, pepper	

Butter a shallow baking dish.   Roll crackers and place a layer on the bottom of dish.   Dot over with bits of butter.   Place a layer of oysters next, adding salt, pepper, and more butter bits.   Mix the milk and oyster juice and pour over all.   Place crumbs and bits of butter on top.   Do not spare the butter, if you would have a tasty dish.

FRIED OYSTERS

Choose large oysters for frying.   Allow six for each person.   Dry them well in a cloth.   Roll in cracker meal, beaten egg diluted with milk, then in fine bread crumbs last.   Place a few at a time in a frying basket, not allowing them to touch each other. Fry in deep hot fat.   Remove as soon as light brown, as long cooking toughens them. Serve on a warm napkin placed on a hot platter. Garnish with lemon slices and parsley sprigs. Tartare Sauce is an almost indispensable accompaniment.

OYSTERS IN GREEN PEPPERS

Cut the stem ends from the peppers. Remove every seed. Cook three minutes in salted water. Place them upright in a buttered baking dish and fill with alternate layers of small oysters and buttered cracker crumbs. Season well with salt and pepper. Place buttered crumbs on top. Bake until brown. Little Neck clams, scallops, or creamed fish may be used similarly.

OYSTERS — "PACIFIC CLUB"

These are baked in the half shell. Allow four oysters for each person. Prepare a mixture of two tablespoons minced green peppers, one third of a cup grated horseradish, one teaspoon lemon juice, and one tablespoon melted butter. Lay the oysters in their half shells on a baking dish. Sprinkle over each a seasoning of salt and pepper, and divide the mixture among them, until each oyster is covered. Lay a thin narrow slice of bacon over each top and bake in hot oven ten minutes.

OYSTER PIE

1 cup flour	5 tablespoons water
½ teaspoon salt	1 or 2 cups oysters
1 teaspoon baking powder	1 cup thick white sauce
4 tablespoons lard	Salt, pepper, onion juice
	Parsley minced

Make a pastry for the pie by sifting the flour, salt, and baking powder. Rub in the shortening and mix to a dough with cold water. Divide into halves. Roll one half to one quarter inch in thickness. Fit it into a deep pie plate.

Clean and look over the oysters, using from one to two cups, according to the depth of the plate. Place a layer on the under crust. Season with the salt, pepper, onion juice, and parsley. Then another layer of oysters until all are used. Pour the white sauce over all. Cut the remainder of the pastry into strips three quarters inch wide and arrange them, lattice fashion, over the top of the pie. Brush over with cold milk. Bake forty-five minutes in a hot oven.

FRIED PICKEREL

Prepare and clean the fish. Cut into pieces for individual serving. Dip each piece in milk, roll in flour, sprinkle with salt. Fry in deep hot fat. Drain on paper. A hot tomato sauce is very good with pickerel.

QUAHOG CAKES — OLD PROVINCETOWN RECIPE

1 dozen quahogs or hard clams, chopped fine	½ teaspoon cream of tartar
	¼ teaspoon soda
½ cup flour	1 egg

Sift together the dry ingredients. Beat the egg and mix in. Add the chopped clams and mold into small flat cakes. Fry on both sides in hot pork fat.

QUAHOG PIE — "ORLEANS"

1 quart of quahogs	1½ teaspoons poultry seasoning
8 common or Boston crackers	
	½ cup melted butter or chicken fat
1 egg	
1 pint milk	Salt

Make a top and bottom pastry crust. Line a custard pie plate. Put the quahogs and crackers through a food chopper. Combine with the remaining ingredients and fill the pie plate. Cover with a vented upper crust. Bake three quarters of an hour in a moderate oven or at 375° F.

THE CAP'N'S QUAHOG PIE — "BASS RIVER"

Biscuit Crust

3 cups flour	2 tablespoons lard
7 level teaspoons baking powder	1 teaspoon salt
Milk to mix	

Filling for Pie

1 quart quahogs	1⅓ cups clam liquor
¼ pound salt pork	5 tablespoons flour
½ cup milk	Salt, pepper

This recipe calls for a deep dish such as is used for Chicken Pie. Make a biscuit crust with the ingredients given. Roll out two crusts. Line the pie dish. Wash, pick over, and chop clams. Cut the salt pork into bits and try out.

Scrape fat and clams into a chowder kettle. Cover with water and simmer two hours. Remove the clams. Make a sauce or gravy of the clam juice, milk, and flour, using enough to fill the dish. Put the clams in and cover with the gravy. Cut a hole in the top crust and place over pie. Bake until light brown. Add more gravy through the vented upper crust if it thickens too much. Bake as for Orleans Pie above.

SALMON STEAKS

The steaks should be cut one inch thick and may be broiled or poached. For broiling, brush the surfaces with oil mixed with salt, pepper, and a little onion juice. Let stand to absorb. Wrap the fish in well-oiled paper and place on a hot, oiled broiler. Cook six to eight minutes on each side, or until tender. Remove paper. Serve with Parsley Butter or Tartare Sauce.

SCALLOPS, BAKED IN SHELLS

Cut the fresh scallops into halves. Pour boiling water over them and let stand five minutes. Drain.

Butter scallop shells. Put in the scallops. Cover them thickly with a mixture of chopped green peppers, grated onion, lemon juice, salt, and pepper. Pour on cream to fill the shells. Place crumbs and bits of butter on top. Bake brown.

SCALLOP CAKES

Follow recipe for Clam Cakes.

BUTTERED SCALLOPS ON TOAST

1 or 2 cups scallops	2 slices onion
1 round tablespoon butter	Minced parsley, salt, pepper
Slices of toasted bread	

Parboil the scallops, drain, and dry well. Melt the butter in a saucepan, add the onion and cook until yellow. Remove the onion. Put in the scallops. Cover with the melted butter and let brown. Season well and serve on hot toast.

CREAMED SCALLOPS

1 cup scallops	1 tablespoon flour
1 tablespoon butter	½ cup rich milk
Salt, parsley	

Parboil the scallops, drain, and dry. Melt butter in a frying pan and sauté the scallops five minutes. Stir in the flour carefully. Then add milk gradually and blend well together. Season and serve on toast or large crackers split. This is a convenient chafing-dish recipe.

CURRIED SCALLOPS

1 quart scallops	1 teaspoon curry powder
Scallop liquor	Salt, pepper
1 tablespoon butter	Juice of ¼ lemon
1 tablespoon flour	

Parboil the scallops. Drain and reserve the liquor. Mix together the butter, flour, and curry powder to make a sauce, adding the scallop liquor gradually. Cook until thick. Season well with salt and pepper. Put in the scallops and add the lemon juice last.

SCALLOPS ESCALLOPED WITH MUSHROOMS

1 quart scallops	2 tablespoons flour
½ cup mushrooms, cut up	1 cup scallop liquor
2 tablespoons butter	1 cup milk or cream
1 small onion	Scallop shells

Parboil the scallops. Drain and cut them into dice. Fry the sliced onion in butter until yellow. Remove onion and put in the mushrooms. Cook five minutes. Blend in the flour. Cook five minutes more. Add the liquor gradually and stir until it thickens. Put in the scallops, and when well heated, place in the buttered shells. Cover with crumbs and bits of butter on top. Bake until brown.

FRIED SCALLOPS

Mix together a few spoonfuls of olive oil, lemon juice, salt, and pepper, in the proportions of a French dressing. Marinate the scallops in this for twenty minutes. Prepare powdered cracker crumbs. Beat an egg and dilute with milk. Roll the scallops in the crumbs, then in egg, then again in crumbs. Heat fat in a deep kettle. Lay a few scallops at a time in a frying basket, not allowing them to touch each other. Fry to a delicate brown. Pour out on paper. Serve on a napkin on a hot platter. Tartare Sauce is the favorite accompaniment.

BAKED SHAD

2 cups bread crumbs	1 tablespoon melted butter
1 egg yolk, beaten	Slices of fat salt pork
1 tablespoon minced onion	Salt, pepper, lemon juice

Remove the scales from the fish and clean. Make a dressing of the bread crumbs, egg yolk, butter, onion, and seasonings. Stuff and sew up the fish. As shad is inclined to be dry, cover the fish with slices of fat salt pork.

Place in a greased baking pan. Dredge the fish with flour, salt, and pepper. Add a cup of boiling water to the pan. Baste with this every ten minutes. When the fish is tender, remove it with the pork scraps, and make a gravy. Brown one or two tablespoons of flour, and add gradually the liquid in the pan. Stir and cook until well combined. In baking shad, allow one hour for each two and one half pounds of fish. Put into a hot oven at first, then reduce heat after the first fifteen minutes.

SHRIMPS, CREAMED WITH PEAS

1 cup shrimps, fresh or canned	4 tablespoons flour
2 cups milk	1 cup green peas, fresh or canned
3 tablespoons butter	1 teaspoon lemon juice

Salt, pepper, paprika

If canned shrimps are used, they should be drained and washed in cold water. Remove the dark intestinal bits. Then dry and cut into pieces. Heat the milk in a double boiler. Make a paste of melted butter and flour and add it to the boiling milk. Stir to make a smooth sauce. Add the shrimps, peas, and seasonings. If a pink sauce is liked, add a few drops of anchovy essence. Serve on toast or crackers.

FISH AND MEAT SAUCES

ANCHOVY SAUCE

Make a White Sauce foundation and add essence of anchovy by teaspoonfuls until the sauce is tinted a delicate pink. A good sauce for crab croquettes.

BROWN SAUCE

1½ cups stock or milk	1 bay leaf
2 slices onion	2 level tablespoons butter
2 slices carrot	2 level tablespoons flour

Simmer stock or milk with the bay leaf, carrot, and onion slices, for ten minutes to obtain the flavor. Brown the flour in a saucepan and blend with the butter. Add the strained stock gradually and cook and stir to a smooth mixture. Season well with salt and pepper. If not brown enough, add a little bottled brown coloring, or Kitchen Bouquet.

BLACK BUTTER SAUCE

Brown slowly three tablespoons of butter in a saucepan with a little salt and pepper; then add a tablespoon of lemon juice or vinegar and let bubble a moment before using.

BREAD SAUCE FOR GAME

¾ cup soft bread crumbs   2 tablespoons butter
1 onion, grated   2 cups milk
Salt, pepper

Place in a double boiler the bread crumbs, milk, onion, and seasonings. Cook half an hour. Then add the butter and beat well. Serve with fried crumbs made by sautéing stale crumbs in butter until light brown.

CAPER SAUCE

1 tablespoon butter   2 cups beef or vegetable broth
¾ tablespoon flour   1 teaspoon vinegar
1 tablespoon capers   Salt, pepper

Melt butter and add flour to make a smooth paste. Mix gradually with the broth and stir to a cream. Put in the vinegar and capers with the seasonings and cook ten minutes. A tablespoon of sour cream is a desirable addition.

CELERY SAUCE

1 cup white sauce   2 cups celery diced
Thin cream as needed

Cook the celery in boiling salted water until soft. Drain and put through a sieve. Mix with a thick white sauce. Heat again in double boiler and thin with cream and bits of butter.

CHEESE SAUCE

2 tablespoons butter   1 cup milk
2 tablespoons flour   ¾ cup cheese

Melt the butter and blend in the flour. Add milk gradually and the cheese grated or cut into bits. Cook until cheese is melted. Season with salt and pepper.

COCKTAIL SAUCE

½ cup tomato catsup
2 tablespoons grated horse-radish
2 tablespoons Worcestershire Sauce

2 tablespoons lemon juice
½ teaspoon salt
A few drops of Tabasco Sauce

Mix well and serve with oysters or other shellfish. Keep on ice until needed.

CURRY SAUCE

1 tablespoon butter
1 onion sliced thin
1½ cups stock or vegetable water

1 heaping teaspoon curry powder
1½ tablespoons flour
Salt, pepper

Melt the butter and cook the onion six minutes. Add a portion of the stock and cook five more minutes. Mix the curry powder with the remainder of the stock and stir until smooth. Combine and let come to a boil. Press through a sieve. Thicken with flour and butter blended. Season to taste. For curried vegetables, replace the stock with a cup of milk or the liquor of the curried vegetable.

DRAWN BUTTER

4 tablespoons butter	2 cups boiling stock or water
2 tablespoons flour	Salt, paprika

Melt two tablespoons of the butter, add the flour, and blend. Pour on the hot stock or water very gradually, while stirring. Season and boil five minutes. When about to serve, beat in the remaining butter.

DUTCH BUTTER

Mix to a cream one tablespoon of butter. Add one teaspoon of lemon juice very gradually while stirring. Season with a little salt.

EGG SAUCE

2 tablespoons butter	1 cup hot fish stock or milk
1½ tablespoons flour	2 hard-boiled eggs
Salt, pepper	

Make a white sauce of butter, flour, and stock or milk. Add seasonings. To each cup of white sauce add two hard-boiled eggs, sliced. A little chopped parsley is sometimes an improvement.

HOT HOLLANDAISE SAUCE

4 egg yolks	1 tablespoon lemon juice
5 tablespoons butter	½ teaspoon salt
¼ cup hot water	

Put the egg yolks into a double boiler and beat, while adding half a tablespoon of butter and the hot water. Stir until creamy. Then add remaining butter by half tablespoons, stirring and beating to incorporate thoroughly. When the mixture thickens, turn it into a cool bowl and stir in the lemon juice slowly and the salt. As the sauce should not reach boiling point, it is better to have the water in the double boiler just under boiling during the making of the sauce.

PARSLEY BUTTER

Melt but do not brown two tablespoons of butter. Stir in two teaspoonfuls of minced parsley. Make in this proportion for a larger quantity.

TARTARE SAUCE — "CHARLEY'S"

¾ cup mayonnaise
1 tablespoon minced parsley

1 teaspoon chopped sweet pickle
½ teaspoon minced onion
1 teaspoon minced capers

Put all the minced savories into a cheesecloth bag and squeeze hard to remove all possible juice, as too much liquid would spoil the mayonnaise. Add the savories to the mayonnaise shortly before serving.

TOMATO SAUCE

6 or 8 fresh tomatoes
1 slice fat salt pork or
1 tablespoon butter

1 chopped onion
1½ tablespoons flour
Sugar, celery salt, etc.

Wash and slice the tomatoes, skin and all, as they are to be strained. Sprinkle with a little salt and pepper. Mince the pork and try out. Cook the onion in this fat, adding a tablespoon or two of any other vegetable, — such as carrots or green peppers. When lightly browned add the tomatoes and a teaspoon of sugar, a bay leaf, a stalk of celery, or a little celery salt. Let all simmer three quarters of an hour. Then rub through a sieve and thicken with the flour dissolved in a little water. Cook and stir until perfectly smooth. Season again if liked.

SPANISH SAUCE

1 can of tomatoes   3 tablespoons butter
2 onions   1 teaspoon salt
2 green peppers   Seasonings

Remove seeds and fiber from green peppers and slice with the onions. Add to melted butter and let them cook ten minutes. Add tomatoes. Boil up once then simmer slowly until vegetables are tender. Tie cloves, sprigs of parsley and celery, with a bay leaf, in a cheesecloth bag and let simmer with them for delicious flavor. Add salt. Remove bag when sauce is cooked.

VINAIGRETTE SAUCE

1½ cups French dressing   2 tablespoons minced white
2 tablespoons minced parsley   onions

Mix well and keep in cool place, but mixtures with oil are kept better outside the ice box as the oil becomes cloudy if chilled for too long a time.

THIN WHITE SAUCE

1 tablespoon butter	1 cup milk or half milk
1 tablespoon flour	and half white stock
½ teaspoon salt	⅛ teaspoon pepper

Put the butter in a saucepan and let it come to a bubble, taking care not to brown. Put in the flour and blend while cooking. Remove from fire and stir in the milk very slowly, beating to keep it smooth. Add seasonings and return to fire to cook until creamy. If a richer sauce is desired, add an egg yolk after removing from fire at the last.

Thicker sauces may be made in proportions of two or three tablespoons each of butter and flour to one cup of milk.

HORSE-RADISH SAUCE — HOT

¼ cup freshly grated	1 cup white sauce
horseradish	2 tablespoons lemon juice or
¼ cup bread crumbs	vinegar
	½ teaspoon salt

Make a white sauce and mix with bread crumbs and horseradish. When thoroughly hot, add the lemon juice or vinegar gradually. Season.

HORSE-RADISH SAUCE — UNCOOKED

3 tablespoons grated horse-radish
1½ tablespoons mild white vinegar or lemon juice

½ teaspoon sugar
½ teaspoon salt
4 tablespoons cream, whipped

Mix all ingredients except the cream. Whip that stiff and beat in at the last.

LOBSTER SAUCE

2 cups Drawn Butter Sauce (*See* "Fish and Meat Sauces")
2 cups lobster meat, diced

1½ tablespoons lemon juice
Lobster shell and claws
1½ pints cold water

Remove the lobster from the shell. Crack the larger pieces of shell and put every scrap of shell and odd bits into the cold water. Boil twenty minutes, then strain. Use this water to make the Drawn Butter Sauce. To this sauce add the lobster meat cut into very small dice, and the lemon juice. If there is a coral, powder it and add to the sauce. A little anchovy essence will give a pinker tinge.

MAÎTRE D'HÔTEL BUTTER

¼ cup butter
1 tablespoon finely minced parsley

1 tablespoon lemon juice
½ teaspoon each, salt and white pepper

Cream the butter and beat with a fork until light. Whip in the parsley and the seasonings. Add the lemon juice very slowly at last. Set in ice box to chill. Very nice with broiled fish or steaks.

MINT SAUCE

1 bunch of fresh mint   ½ cup mild vinegar
¾ cup water   ⅛ teaspoon salt
          ¼ cup sugar

Shred the mint fine. Place in a saucepan with sugar and water. Boil slowly ten minutes. Add vinegar and remove from fire. Let stand a half hour before using.

MUSHROOM SAUCE

Make a good brown sauce. Sauté in butter half a cup of mushrooms which have been cut into halves. When heated through, add to the brown sauce. If canned mushrooms are used, add a tablespoon of the liquor in making the sauce and let simmer ten minutes.

OYSTER CURRY SAUCE

½ pint small oysters   2 tablespoons flour
Oyster liquor   2 tablespoons butter
1½ cups milk   1 teaspoon curry powder
          Salt, pepper

Heat the oysters in their own juice until plump. Strain the liquor and heat with milk in a double boiler. Melt butter and blend in the flour. Add the curry powder and let cook. Stir in the hot liquid and beat smooth. Add oysters and season to taste.

OLIVE SAUCE FOR GAME

Boil twenty-four queen olives for a half hour. Then pit and chop them. Make a brown sauce with two tablespoons of minced onions and add the chopped olives while hot.

FISH AND POULTRY STUFFINGS

CHESTNUT STUFFING

1 quart of chestnuts
2 cups bread or cracker crumbs
½ cup butter, melted

2 tablespoons cream
1 teaspoon salt
⅛ teaspoon pepper

Boil the chestnuts gently half an hour. Drain and cover with cold water, when the shells will be easily removed. Mash the chestnuts and mix with the cream and one half the butter. Season well. Add the bread crumbs and remaining butter.

OYSTER STUFFING

2 cups soft, stale bread crumbs
⅓ cup butter or oil
1 cup drained oysters

1 teaspoon Bell's poultry dressing
Nutmeg, salt, pepper
1 tablespoon chopped celery

Melt the butter and mix with bread crumbs. Scald the oysters, drain, and cut into pieces. Save the oyster juice and mix in. Add the seasonings and stir well together.

Minced clams may be used in the same way when oysters are not available.

FISH STUFFING

2 cups soft bread crumbs
1½ tablespoons butter or
 oil
1 onion, minced

1 teaspoon minced capers
 and pickles
¼ cup milk or stock
Salt, pepper, mace

Melt the butter and fry the onion.   Soak the bread crumbs in milk until absorbed.   Add the seasonings, melted butter, and onions.   Baking modifies the seasoning, so a rather high seasoning is desirable.

EGGS

EGGS WITH BLACK BUTTER

3 tablespoons butter   1 tablespoon vinegar
Salt, pepper

Brown the butter carefully in an omelet pan. Season with salt and pepper. Add the vinegar and mix well. Draw to a cooler part of stove and break eggs into the liquid. Cover and cook slowly until the eggs are set. Pour remaining liquid over them. They may be cooked very nicely in the oven by pouring the black butter, as soon as prepared, into individual ramekin dishes. Break an egg into each one carefully and place in the oven for eight or ten minutes.

POACHED EGGS, WITH CHEESE SAUCE

Use only fresh eggs for poaching, as the yolks must remain unbroken. Rings for poaching are a convenience. French cooks have a way of whirling the boiling water with the handle of a long spoon until an eddy is formed. Into the center of this eddy the egg is dropped and the circular motion makes the poached egg beautifully round.

Butter the bottom of a shallow enamel saucepan. Put in boiling water just deep enough to cover a dropped egg. Add half a tablespoon of salt and let boil a moment. Break an egg into a cup and slip it gently into the boiling water. Do this quickly until all the eggs are used. Draw the pan away from the direct heat after the eggs are in. The water should not quite boil though it must be kept close to it. In about three minutes the eggs will be covered with a thin film and the white, "set." Lift each egg carefully, draining off the water, and slip it onto buttered toast. Pour a cup and a half of Cheese Sauce around the slices. (See "Sauces.")

POACHED EGGS IN MILK

Scald the milk with a little salt. Drop in the eggs and keep the milk hot but not boiling until the whites are set. Remove to toast and pour the milk as it is, or slightly thickened, over the toast.

EGGS POACHED IN CHICKEN BROTH

Season chicken broth well with salt and pepper. Proceed as with plain poached eggs. Mix a little cornstarch with water until dissolved. Remove the eggs to hot toast and thicken the broth with the cornstarch. Boil up once and pour over the toast.

PLAIN OR FRENCH OMELET

The omelet pan should be kept for omelets alone. Scour it briskly with salt before using, to be sure of a smooth surface. A four-egg omelet is better than a larger one. If more than two or three people are to be served make several small omelets. Break the eggs into a bowl with a pinch of salt, a speck of pepper, and one teaspoon of cold water. Beat with a fork until well broken up. Place the scoured pan over a slow fire. Put in one tablespoon of butter for each egg. Let it run over the whole surface of the pan but take care not to brown it. Turn in the eggs and shake gently as they spread over the pan. When the omelet begins to adhere to the bottom of the pan, do not disturb this foundation, but with a fork continue to pick up the soft part while turning the pan about to allow the bottom to brown evenly. While the omelet is still creamy, fold it over twice with a spatula, shaping pointed ends and rounded center. Cook another minute, then hold a warm platter in the left hand over the omelet and quickly invert the pan, slipping the omelet upon the platter.

PARSLEY OMELET

Mix the eggs, salt, pepper, and water in a bowl as for a plain omelet. Add to them a full tablespoon of parsley, minced fine. Beat well, then let stand a half hour before cooking and finishing as for Plain Omelet.

CHEESE OMELET

Grate two tablespoons of cheese. Make a plain omelet and sprinkle the cheese over the hot surface just before folding it. Watercress or sprigs of parsley make a desirable garnish.

ASPARAGUS OMELET

Drain a can of asparagus tips or use fresh ones, cooked. Let them simmer in melted butter until thoroughly hot and well flavored. Then fold in as above. If preferred, the tips may be creamed and poured about the hot omelet on the serving platter.

MINCED HAM OMELET

Mince four tablespoons of boiled ham. Simmer in a little melted butter until thoroughly heated. Then add to the plain omelet before folding.

MUSHROOM OMELET

Peel and cut into pieces of even size the caps and stems of mushrooms. Heat three tablespoons of butter in a saucepan and sauté the mushrooms until the butter has been absorbed. Season with salt and pepper. Pour over the omelet and serve.

SPANISH OMELET

Make a sauce by melting a tablespoon of butter and cooking in it for five minutes one chopped onion, two seeded and minced green peppers, and two cups drained, canned tomatoes or chopped fresh ones. Cook slowly about twenty minutes or until the sauce thickens. Season with salt and pepper. Use a portion of the sauce in the fold of the omelet and pour the remainder around it.

PUFFY OMELET

3 eggs separated	2 tablespoons butter
3 tablespoons milk	Salt, pepper

Separate the yolks from the whites. Mix the yolks with the milk and beat up light. Beat the whites until stiff. Cut the whites into the yolk and milk mixture. Season. Turn into the melted butter in an omelet pan and cook slowly. When well puffed place in a hot oven three minutes. Remove, fold, and serve.

EGG TIMBALES

1 cup milk	4 eggs, separated
1¼ tablespoons flour	1 tablespoon chopped parsley
1 tablespoon butter	Celery salt, pepper

Make a paste of the flour and milk. Melt the butter and add with the seasonings. Beat the egg yolks until lemon colored and stir in. Whip the whites to a stiff froth and fold in with a fork. Butter small cups or timbale molds and fill with the mixture. Set to bake for fifteen or twenty minutes in a pan with hot water reaching nearly to the tops of the cups. Let bake until set, then turn out on a warm platter and serve with cheese or tomato sauce.

CLAM OMELET — "BASS RIVER"

6 medium-sized hard clams	1 tablespoon flour
½ cup milk	3 eggs, separated
1 tablespoon butter	Salt, pepper

Chop the clams rather fine. Make a white sauce of the butter, flour, and milk. Beat yolks of the eggs until lemon colored. Mix with the white sauce and the clams. Beat the whites stiff and fold in. Melt the butter in an omelet pan and turn in the mixture. Cook until it rises and is a light brown on the bottom — discovered by gently lifting one edge of the omelet with a spatula. Place in the oven to cook the top slightly. Crease, fold, and serve hot.

CREAMED EGGS

Butter a shallow baking dish. Heat one cup of milk in the dish. Break eggs into the milk and let poach, covered closely, until set. Do not place them where they will boil hard, but allow to simmer very gently. When the eggs are set, season with a little salt, cover with cream, and place in the oven five minutes. Sprinkle with minced parsley and serve.

SCRAMBLED EGGS

Beat four or five fresh eggs with a fork lightly. Melt one tablespoon of butter in a saucepan, and when hot, pour in the eggs. Pick them up constantly with the fork as they cook, and season well with salt and pepper, adding another teaspoon of butter as the first is absorbed. For eggs scrambled with milk, allow half a cup of milk to four eggs, and proceed as before. Serve on a hot platter garnished with triangular pieces of thin toast.

BREADS

BACON MUFFINS

5 or 6 slices bacon
2 tablespoons bacon fat
1 tablespoon sugar
1 egg well beaten

1 cup milk
2 cups flour
4 teaspoons baking powder
   (level)
½ teaspoon salt

Fry the bacon until crisp. Cut into very small bits. Mix together the melted fat and sugar, milk, and beaten egg. Sift salt, baking powder, and flour. Add the minced bacon. Combine mixtures. Pour into greased muffin tins. Bake in moderately hot oven, or at 400° F.

BAKING-POWDER BISCUIT

2 cups bread flour
5 level teaspoons baking powder

4 tablespoons butter
¾ to 1 cup milk
1 teaspoon salt

Sift together the flour, salt, and baking powder. Work in the butter with the finger tips. Add milk gradually, mixing it in with a silver knife. Roll out lightly on a floured board and cut with small cutter. Brush over the tops with milk after placing in a greased pan. Bake in quick oven, or at 450° F. for fifteen minutes.

BAKING-POWDER CHEESE BISCUIT

To the above recipe add one egg well beaten, and replace the butter with two rounded tablespoons grated cheese and one tablespoon butter only. Stir in the cheese just before mixing with the milk. These are delicious with a salad course.

BLUEBERRY MUFFINS

2 cups flour	¾ cup milk
3 teaspoons baking powder	1 tablespoon butter, melted
1 tablespoon sugar	2 eggs
1 teaspoon salt	1 cup berries

Sift together the dry ingredients. Add milk slowly. Then the well-beaten eggs and melted butter. Dry the berries and dust with flour. Add after mixture is well beaten. Bake in well-greased tins about twenty minutes in a moderate oven, or at 400° F.

BROWN BREAD — "SATURDAY NIGHT"

1 cup Indian or corn meal	1 teaspoon soda
2 cups Graham flour	1 cup molasses
1 teaspoon salt	2 cups hot water

Mix well all the dry ingredients. Add the hot water to the molasses. Pour into the middle of the mixture and stir until smooth. Steam three hours in a tightly covered tin.

RAISIN BROWN BREAD

1 cup white corn meal	1 teaspoon soda
1 cup rye flour	½ cup molasses
1 cup Graham flour	2 cups sour milk
1 teaspoon salt	1 cup seeded raisins

Sift the soda with flour. Mix all ingredients together in order given. Cut the raisins into halves. Thin the batter with milk or water until it can be poured readily. Steam three hours.

BLUEBERRY BREAKFAST CAKE

½ cup sugar	¾ teaspoon cream of tartar
1 rounded tablespoon butter	⅜ teaspoon soda
1 egg	½ teaspoon salt
1½ cups flour	½ cup milk
1 heaping cup blueberries	

Cream together butter and sugar. Break in the egg and beat well. Sift twice together the flour, cream of tartar, soda, and salt. Add the dry ingredients alternately to the first mixture with the milk. Beat well. Dry and flour the berries and stir in last. Bake in moderately hot oven — 400° F. — and cut into squares while hot.

CORN MEAL MUSH — "HASTY PUDDING"

Old-fashioned "Hasty Pudding" was made by stirring a cup of granulated corn meal into a pint of rapidly boiling water, adding a pinch of salt, and boiling quickly until the pudding thickened. It is far more wholesome, however, to mix the meal to a paste with cold water and then add it to the boiling water so gradually that the boiling does not cease. After it has thickened, remove to a double boiler and allow it to steam for several hours until thoroughly cooked.

FRIED CORN MEAL MUSH

If planning to fry the mush when cold, add flour to the corn meal when cooking. This makes it easier to slice when cold. Empty baking-powder tins make excellent molds. They should be rinsed inside with cold water before packing the cooked mush down inside. Smooth off the top. When ready to use, grease and heat a griddle, using salt pork fat or oil and lightly flour the slices before placing them on the hot griddle. New Orleans molasses was the preferred old-time accompaniment. Maple syrup is also good.

BUCKWHEAT CAKES

¼ yeast cake	3 cups buckwheat flour
½ cup warm water	1 tablespoon molasses
2 cups scalded milk	¼ teaspoon soda
½ teaspoon salt	2 tablespoons warm water

These must be started the night before in order to rise. Break yeast cake into bits and dissolve in the warm water. When the milk is lukewarm, add the salt and buckwheat flour gradually to make a soft batter. Beat three minutes. Set in warm place overnight. In the morning add the molasses. Dissolve soda in warm water and stir in. Beat two minutes. Grease and heat a griddle piping hot. Drop the batter by spoonfuls, watching until bubbles appear on the cakes and the edges turn brown. Then turn over carefully and brown other side. Serve on hot plates with plenty of butter and New Orleans molasses or maple syrup.

CORN MEAL GRIDDLE CAKES

1½ cups sour milk	1 teaspoon salt
1 teaspoon soda	½ cup white flour
1 egg, beaten	Yellow corn meal to make a
1 tablespoon sugar	thin batter

Dissolve the soda in the milk. Mix with remaining ingredients and beat smooth. Drop from a spoon on a hot greased griddle and brown both sides.

FALMOUTH BUNS — OLD RECIPE

4 cups bread flour	½ cup butter
1 cup sugar	1 cup seedless raisins or currants
1 yeast cake	1 teaspoon lemon extract
⅓ cup warm water	Soda, size of a pea
1⅓ cups scalded milk	2 tablespoons molasses
⅛ teaspoon salt	2 tablespoons melted butter

Scald milk, add the butter, and allow to become tepid. Dissolve the yeast cake in the warm water. Mix together the flour, sugar, and salt. Pour over them the dissolved yeast. Mix rather soft with the milk and allow to rise overnight, or for several hours. Dissolve the soda in the warm water and stir in. Add raisins and flavoring. Mix thoroughly. Roll out on a floured board. Cut with a small cookie cutter. Set to rise again. This requires time on account of the fruit.

Bake in a medium oven, or at 350° F. On removing from oven, brush tops with the melted butter and molasses.

CINNAMON ROLLS

2 cups milk, heated	Flour for a soft dough
2 tablespoons butter	1 cup brown sugar
¾ cup sugar — white	½ cup melted butter
2 eggs	½ teaspoon salt
1 yeast cake	Cinnamon

Mix butter and sugar. Pour over them the hot milk. Let cool. Beat eggs light. Dissolve yeast cake in warm water and stir both in. Add flour to make a soft dough. Let rise overnight. In the morning, turn out on a floured board and pull out flat. Make a mixture of brown sugar, melted butter, and a generous quantity of powdered cinnamon. Spread this on the dough. Then roll it up like a jelly roll. Slice about three quarters of an inch thick to form buns. Place them close together in a buttered pan. Let rise another hour. Brush over the tops with melted butter. Bake in a moderate oven, or at 350° F.

NUT BRAN MUFFINS

1 cup bran	1 egg
½ cup Graham or entire wheat flour	2 tablespoons molasses
½ teaspoon salt	1 cup milk
2 teaspoons baking powder	¼ cup seeded raisins
	¼ cup walnut meats

Beat the egg thoroughly. Add the molasses, and beat again. Sift baking powder into flour and stir in. Add the salt and bran. Cut raisins and nut meats into bits, but not too small, and mix in. Bake in buttered muffin tins in a hot oven, or at 400° F.

SOUR MILK CORN BREAD

¾ cup corn meal	½ teaspoon salt
¾ cup white flour	1 cup thick sour milk
1 tablespoon sugar	1 egg, slightly beaten
½ teaspoon soda	

Sift together the dry ingredients. Beat in the egg and the sour milk. Pour into a greased tin or separate muffin rings. Start the oven at 350° F., finishing at 400° F. The bread will shrink from the sides of the tin when done.

SWEET MILK CORN BREAD

1 cup corn meal	¼ cup butter or substitute
1 cup white flour	¾ teaspoon salt
2 tablespoons sugar	1 egg, well beaten
3 teaspoons baking powder	1 cup sweet milk

Sift and mix together the dry ingredients. Melt the butter. Combine mixtures. Bake twenty to thirty minutes in a moderately hot oven, or at 400° F.

CLARA'S GRIDDLE CAKES

1½ cups whole wheat flour   2 cups sour milk
1 teaspoon soda   ½ teaspoon salt

Sift the soda with the flour. Add salt. Beat in the sour milk thoroughly. Grease the hot griddle with the rind of fat salt pork. Drop the thin batter from the tip of a spoon and brown both sides very lightly. These cakes should be very light and thin as wafers. Very delicious with small sausages for Sunday morning breakfast.

OLD NANTUCKET GRIDDLE CAKES

1 cup stale bread crumbs   1 egg
1 cup sour milk   1 tablespoon sugar
½ teaspoon saleratus (soda)   White flour, salt

Soak the bread in milk until soft. Add the saleratus, beaten egg, and sugar. If the griddle cakes are liked quite brown, a little molasses may be added. Stir in enough flour to make a batter easily dropped from tip of a spoon. Grease griddle with pork rind to prevent burning.

RICE GRIDDLE CAKES

1½ cups cold boiled rice	1 tablespoon sugar
2 eggs	2 cups white flour
2 cups milk	2 teaspoons baking powder

½ teaspoon salt

Mix ingredients and beat well. Drop on hot greased griddle and brown lightly.

QUICK NUT BISCUIT

⅓ cup butter	½ cup pecan nuts
¾ cup brown sugar, sifted	Baking-powder dough

Make a dough as for Baking Powder Biscuit. Roll out half an inch thick. Cream the butter and brown sugar and spread on the dough. Sprinkle on the chopped nut meats and roll up like a jelly roll. Then cut into slices one inch thick. Bake in greased muffin tins in fairly hot oven, or at 400° F.

BARNSTABLE NUT MUFFINS

2 cups bread flour	1 tablespoon lard
½ cup sugar	1 egg well beaten
4 teaspoons baking powder	1 extra egg yolk
1 tablespoon butter	1 cup milk

½ cup nut meats, chopped

Sift together flour, sugar, and baking powder. Work in the lard and butter. Add the beaten egg and egg yolk, the milk by degrees, a pinch of salt, and the nut meats. Pour into buttered muffin tins and let stand twenty minutes. Bake in moderate oven, or at 400° F. They are good hot or cold.

RAISED MUFFINS

½ cup boiling water	1 egg well beaten
½ cup scalded milk	¼ yeast cake
2 tablespoons sugar	¼ cup tepid water
2 tablespoons shortening	1 teaspoon salt
2½ cups flour	

Mix together salt, sugar, and shortening. Pour the hot milk and water over them. When cool add well-beaten egg. Dissolve yeast cake in tepid water and stir in. Then the sifted flour. Beat all together well. Set to rise overnight in warm place. In the morning beat once more. Grease muffin tins and fill two thirds full. Let rise again. Bake in hot oven, or at 400° F., for a half hour.

TEA SCONES — "CHATHAM"

2 cups pastry flour	2 tablespoons shortening
½ teaspoon salt	1 egg beaten light
4 teaspoons baking powder	⅔ cup milk

Sift together dry ingredients. Cut in the shortening with a knife. Mix beaten egg with milk. Make a dough. Turn out on floured board and pull to a round about half an inch thick. Cut into squares, then across to make triangles. Brush over with melted butter and place in buttered pan short distances apart and bake fifteen minutes. They are sometimes baked on top of stove on a hot griddle, turning to brown both sides. To serve, split and toast, buttering while hot.

FRUIT SCONES

Add a quarter of a cup of sugar to above recipe for Tea Scones and use the yolks of two eggs in place of one whole egg.   Put in at last half a cup washed and floured currants or Sultana raisins.   If preferred, the scones may be cut into large rounds instead of triangles.

SHREDDED WHEAT BREAD

2 shredded wheat biscuit	1/4 teaspoon soda
2 cups boiling water	1 tablespoon lard, heaping
1/3 cup sugar	1 yeast cake
1/2 cup molasses	1/2 cup warm water
1 cup scalded milk	1 tablespoon salt

Flour to knead

Soak the biscuit in the boiling water until soft. Dissolve soda in the milk and the yeast cake in the warm water.   Mix all ingredients together.   Add flour enough to knead.   Let rise overnight.   Place in bread pans.   Set in warm place.   Bake, when raised to level of the pans, in a moderately hot oven at 450° until brown, then reduce to 370° F. until finished.

NUT BREAD NUMBER I

1 cup white flour	2 tablespoons sugar
2 cups whole wheat or Graham	1/2 teaspoon salt
	1/2 cup molasses
1 scant teaspoon soda	1 1/2 cups sour milk

1 cup walnut meats, chopped

Sift together the dry ingredients. Stir in the molasses and sour milk. Add walnut meats last. This is a moist and delicious bread for sandwiches. Bake about forty-five minutes in a greased bread tin, in moderate oven, or at 350° F.

NUT BREAD NUMBER II

1 cup bran flour	2 beaten eggs
1 cup whole wheat flour	1 cup milk
1 cup white flour	1 cup walnut meats
2 tablespoons baking powder	1 cup seeded raisins or
1 cup brown sugar	dates

⅛ teaspoon salt

Mix the dry ingredients together, then eggs, milk, nut meats, and raisins. Bake one hour in a slow oven, or at 300° F.

PARKER HOUSE ROLLS

2 cups milk scalded	1 level teaspoon salt
2 tablespoons sugar	1 yeast cake
2 tablespoons butter	¼ cup tepid water

Bread flour

Mix together the sugar, salt, and butter. Pour over them the scalded milk. Cool. Dissolve yeast cake in tepid water and add to the cooled mixture. Sift in three cups bread flour. Mix well and set aside to rise about one and a half hours. Then beat down with a spoon. Add more flour — about two and a half cups but not enough to make a stiff dough. The softer the dough the more delicate the rolls. Let rise again until doubled in bulk. Turn out on floured board and cut with small cutter. Crease with a knife. Brush over creased side with melted butter. Fold over. Let rise again. Bake in hot oven, or at 450° F., until brown, then reduce heat to 350° F. and finish baking.

TRUSTY POPOVERS

1 cup flour	1 cup milk
¼ teaspoon salt	1 teaspoon melted butter
	1 egg

Butter iron popover forms and place in oven to become hot. Sift together the flour and salt. Beat the egg very light. Add gradually to the flour. Stir in melted butter. Beat hard two minutes with rotary egg beater until the mixture is full of air. Fill hot forms three quarters full and bake in oven with increasing heat about twenty-five minutes. Set the oven at 500° F. until they puff, then reduce to 350° F. and finish baking.

WAFFLES — "HOUSE ON THE SANDS"

2 cups flour	2 eggs, separated
3 teaspoons baking powder	2 cups milk
¾ teaspoon salt	1 tablespoon melted butter

Mix dry ingredients and add milk slowly. Beat egg yolks light and stir in. Then the melted butter, and last the stiffly beaten whites, folded in. The batter must not be thick but thin enough to spread quickly over the hot buttered iron without running. Brown both sides and serve with maple syrup.

RICE WAFFLES

2 scant cups flour	¼ teaspoon salt
4 teaspoons baking powder	⅔ cup cold cooked rice

Mix these ingredients together well then add: One and one-third cups milk with yolk of an egg well beaten, a tablespoon of melted butter, and last, the egg white stiffly beaten.

SANDWICHES

CHICKEN AND NUT

Chop the meat of cold chicken with English walnut meats. Season with salt and paprika. Moisten with cream. Spread on thin slices of rye bread well buttered.

CLUB SANDWICHES — "BOURNDALE"

Use two slices of lightly browned toast for each service. Spread one slice with mayonnaise and cover with a crisp lettuce leaf. Place a thin slice of cold chicken on the lettuce, then two strips of freshly fried bacon on the chicken; another lettuce leaf, and the second slice of toast also spread with mayonnaise to complete the sandwich. Press together firmly and cut obliquely to form two triangles. All ingredients must be at hand when making this sandwich, as the toast and bacon must be hot when served.

ROLLED WATERCRESS SANDWICHES

Bread must be very fresh in order to make successful rolled sandwiches. Trim the crusts from a loaf of freshly baked white bread. Cream half a cup of butter or soften it sufficiently to spread easily. Butter a slice and then cut as thin as possible with a very sharp knife. The slices should be about three inches square when trimmed. Place a leaf of watercress on a slice, with the green leaf projecting beyond the edge and the stem on the bread. Roll the square and wrap in waxed paper until needed. Plain rolled sandwiches are sometimes tied with narrow ribbon.

OPEN SANDWICHES

These are attractive for afternoon teas. A variety of cutters may be bought — star-shaped, heart, diamond, and half moon. The bread may be white or brown. The fillings are innumerable but cream cheese combinations are always satisfactory. An attractive round sandwich is made by cutting rounds of fresh bread with a round biscuit cutter. Spread with well-seasoned cream cheese. Cut rounds for the top with a doughnut cutter of the same size as the biscuit cutter. This leaves little open spaces in the middle. Fill these with chopped stuffed olives.

SANDWICH FILLINGS

Good sandwich fillings for tea or picnic sandwiches are made with the following combinations :
Chopped hard-boiled egg, mayonnaise, and lettuce
Egg and chopped olives

Egg and chopped beets

Thinly sliced American cheese and mustard

Creamed cheese, salted, with chopped walnut meats

Creamed pimento cheese on freshly toasted bread

Orange marmalade and creamed cheese

Minced ham and chopped pickle

Chopped cucumber and salad dressing

Minced green pepper with a little minced onion

Mashed sardines and salad dressing

Chopped bacon and creamed cheese

Hot minced chicken

Roquefort cheese and sliced tomato

Chopped dates and raisins with a little grated orange rind and juice

TOAST

EGG AND CHEESE TOAST

Make well-seasoned scrambled eggs with milk.
Toast a slice of bread for each service, and spread
with Chutney or tomato catsup. Heap the
scrambled eggs on the toast and cover thickly with
grated cheese. Set into the oven to brown. Garnish with narrow strips of green pepper alternating
with strips of pimentos.

CELERY TOAST

2 cups celery diced	3 cups hot water or
⅓ cup flour	vegetable stock
¼ cup milk	Salt, pepper

Cook the celery — which may be the coarse parts
of the stalks — in hot water or stock for half an hour,
or until tender. Mix the flour to a paste with the
milk, add the seasonings, and stir in. Continue
stirring until thick. Then simmer ten or fifteen
minutes. Serve on slices of toast. Garnish with
celery tips.

CINNAMON TOAST

Make a mixture of three parts sugar to one of
powdered cinnamon and spread generously on freshly

buttered slices of toast. Honey is very good spread over the toast before the sugar and cinnamon are added.

CREAM TOAST

2 cups scalded milk	1 tablespoon butter
3 tablespoons flour	Salt
¼ cup cold water to mix	Toasted slices of bread

Make a smooth paste of the flour and cold water. Stir into the hot milk until it thickens. Cook in double boiler over hot water fifteen minutes. Add salt and the butter and pour over hot toasted bread. If very stale bread is used, dip the slices in and out of hot salted water quickly while the cream is cooking.

MILK TOAST

Scald three cups milk with two tablespoons butter and a pinch of salt. Place the toast in this hot mixture until heated through. Pour remainder of milk over the toast after removal to warm platter.

FRENCH TOAST

2 eggs	¼ teaspoon salt
2 tablespoons sugar	1 cup milk
5 or 6 slices stale bread	

Beat the eggs slightly with a fork and stir in the salt, sugar, and milk, slowly. Soak the slices of bread in the mixture. Brown on both sides on hot

greased griddle.   Sprinkle with sugar after removal
to warm dish.

TOAST FOR GAME

Remove crusts from several slices of stale bread.
Shape as desired, triangles, squares, etc.   After game
has been cooked and removed from the pan, bring
the fat remaining to a boil on top of stove.   Sauté
the toast in this fat until crisp and brown.

MEATS

ASPIC JELLY

1 large can consommé soup   2 tablespoons gelatine
Seasonings

This is a very convenient quick way of making aspic for cold meats. Put over the fire the consommé, adding as seasoning bits of celery, a teaspoon of lemon juice, and two or three slices of onion. Simmer for a half hour. Soak the gelatine five minutes in water to cover. Boil up the consommé, add the gelatine, and stir until dissolved. Strain and cool. If to be used for jellied meats pour it, while hot, over cut-up cold meat or fish. If preferred plain, cut into squares and serve with the meat.

TO COOK BACON

Instead of broiling the bacon over the fire, place the strips on the hot broiler over a dripping pan and set into a hot oven until crisp. If preferred, bacon may be pan-broiled on top of stove by tilting the pan over a poker or iron so that the hot fat runs away from the cooking bacon. Remove the fat with a spoon as it gathers. Turn the slices often to cook evenly.

CALF'S LIVER AND BACON

Let the liver stand five minutes in boiling water. Drain and wipe dry. Cut into serving pieces, removing the thin outer skin. Dip into flour, salt, and pepper. Cook the slices of bacon until crisp. Remove from fat and keep hot. Fry the liver in the bacon fat. For gravy, remove liver and add to the fat — two tablespoons flour stirred into half a cup hot water, and a tablespoon of vinegar. Make gravy thinner or thicker by adding vinegar or flour. Serve the bacon and liver in overlapping slices on a hot platter and pour the gravy over them.

NEW ENGLAND BOILED DINNER

Corned beef is used for this. Order a piece of the brisket weighing about five pounds. Cover with cold water and boil fifteen minutes. Skim the water. Remove kettle to lower heat and simmer very slowly about five hours or until the meat is tender. During the last hour of cooking, add a cabbage cut into quarters, peeled turnips, potatoes, and carrots. If beets are desired they must be cooked in a separate dish. Skim the fat from the water and use in making hash next day. Place the beef on a warm platter with the vegetables surrounding it.

CORNED BEEF HASH

Take equal parts of cold corned beef and cold boiled potatoes. Chop or run through the food chopper, adding a little green pepper and onion for flavor. Season with salt and pepper. Melt a generous spoonful of fat or butter in a saucepan and add the hash. Turn it over with a knife while cooking. Let brown on the bottom and fold over like an omelet. Serve tomato catsup or piccalilli with it.

CHICKEN À LA KING

Breast of cooked chicken	1 green pepper
1½ cups thick white sauce	Yolks 2 eggs
1 cup mushrooms	Juice ½ lemon
Salt, paprika, mustard	

Cut the breast into cubes. Peel mushrooms and cut into pieces. Parboil them six minutes in boiling water. Seed and dice the pepper and parboil. Heat the cream sauce in double boiler. Add the egg yolks, seasonings, mushrooms, chicken, and green pepper. Bring nearly to a boil and simmer ten minutes. Serve on toast.

FRIED CHICKEN AND CREAM GRAVY

Cut a large broiler into quarters. Put into iron spider with a cup of water, two or three slices of onion, a bay leaf, and cook about an hour, closely covered. Add salt, pepper, and more water if needed. If the chicken is tender, remove from fire, and pour liquid into a separate bowl. Place three tablespoons of butter in the spider, sprinkle the chicken with salt and pepper and fry in the butter. Remove chicken. Add three tablespoons of flour to the fat, a cup of the reserved liquid, and a half cup of cream. Stir and cook until it thickens. Serve chicken on a warm platter with the sauce poured over it.

CHICKEN SMOTHERED IN OYSTERS

A small young chicken is necessary for this. Split it down the back, and lay it, skin side up, in a roasting pan. Rub surface with butter, salt, and pepper. Pour one cup boiling water into the pan. Cover closely and cook in oven an hour or more until tender. Then pour over it one cup of cream, and one pint of small oysters, drained and cleaned. Cover again and cook fifteen minutes. Remove chicken to a hot platter and pour oysters and sauce over it.

DOLLY'S CHICKEN FRICASSEE

Cut a fowl into pieces. Dredge with flour and salt. Fry brown in bacon fat. Put into a kettle and cover with warm water. Simmer four hours. Peel six or eight onions of uniform size. After the chicken has cooked two hours, place the onions on top to steam. Be sure to keep them out of the water.

When tender, take up the onions.   Place the chicken in middle of a warm platter;   arrange the onions around it.   Thicken the liquid with a little flour mixed with water.   Make a gravy and pour over. If available, add half a pound of mushrooms sautéed in butter.   Dumplings are sometimes liked with this dish.

ROAST CHICKEN AND SAUSAGES

Select a four-pound chicken. Fill with celery stuffing.   Sew and truss.   Rub all surfaces with oil or softened butter.   Dredge with flour.   Put into a hot oven, then reduce heat and cook slowly about two hours.   Baste often with the fat in the pan. Serve, surrounded by sausages, which have been pricked with a large needle and baked in a pan with five or six tablespoons of boiling water.

CHICKEN LOAF

1½ cups chopped chicken remnants	1 tablespoon Worcestershire Sauce
½ cup bacon minced	1½ teaspoons salt
½ cup minced onion	½ teaspoon pepper
1 cup thick white sauce	1 egg well beaten
1 cup fine white bread crumbs	2½ cups cold boiled rice

Brown the bacon and onion.   Take out the bacon and simmer onions in the fat until tender, without browning them.   Add all remaining ingredients and mix well.   Grease and lightly flour a bread tin.

Pack the mixture into it and set the pan into a larger one containing hot water. Bake one hour in a slow oven — 325° F. Remove large pan with water and continue baking the loaf fifteen minutes longer. Serve hot or cold.

CHICKEN LIVERS AND BACON

Wash and dry the livers. Cut them into halves. Cut strips of bacon into pieces of same size. Arrange them alternately and not too close together on long metal skewers. Put the ends of the skewers across a baking pan so no fat will be lost and bake in a fairly hot oven twenty minutes. The bacon will be crisp, but not dark. Serve on the skewers or remove to slices of toast.

STUFFED LAMB CHOPS — " YARMOUTH "

Sear one side only of each chop. Make a dressing of bread crumbs, minced onion, butter, and Bell's seasoning. Form a mound of the dressing on top of each chop on the seared side. Bake about half an hour in hot oven or at 450° F. Use the oven at the same time for baking potatoes in their jackets or squash in the shell.

BAKED HAM IN CIDER

Scrape the ham and wash thoroughly in hot water. Soak overnight in cold water. Rinse in the morning.

Place in a kettle with fresh cold water to cover and bring slowly to boiling point, skimming off the fat as it appears on the surface. Add to the water six cloves, a bay leaf, a few allspice berries, a red pepper pod if you have it, and simmer slowly until the ham is tender. Take care not to let it boil hard at any time. Remove kettle from fire and let ham cool in the liquor. Drain. Remove loose bits of fat or skin. Pour over the ham one and a half quarts of cider and let soak overnight. Then dry it and stick cloves all over the surface. Make a mixture of bread crumbs and one cup of brown sugar. Brush the ham with beaten egg, then cover with the sugar and fine crumbs. Place in a baking pan; pour the cider over it, and bake until brown in a slow oven or at 325° F. Baste with the cider in the pan occasionally. This is delicious, hot or cold.

HAM WITH PINEAPPLE ROUNDS

Take a slice of frying ham about one inch thick. Soak, if salt, in scalding water for half an hour. Place in a spider with pepper and made mustard. Pour over it one teaspoon vinegar. Fry quickly, turning often. Remove ham and flavor gravy with one teaspoon sugar, one tablespoon cooking sherry, or homemade wine. Sear slices of pineapple in butter. Serve on the platter with the ham. Boil the gravy up once and pour over the ham.

COMBINATION CHOPS — "SOUTH DENNIS"

Sear pork chops on both sides. On each chop place one slice of onion, one slice of tomato, and a little minced green pepper. Season well with salt and pepper. Scatter over all one tablespoon uncooked rice. Add water to cover and to form a gravy. Bake in a hot oven or 350° F. until the rice is soft. The oven may be used at the same time to bake potatoes.

HAM IN MILK

1 slice of ham cut	⅓ cup water
2 or 3 inches thick	2 tablespoons brown sugar
⅓ cup flour	1 teaspoon dry mustard
	Milk to cover

Parboil the ham fifteen minutes to remove the salt. Make a paste of the flour, water, sugar, and mustard. Cover the top of the ham with this and place in a baking pan. Pour in milk to cover the edges of the ham. Bake slowly — 325° F. — until tender. Add more milk if it dries out. Serve with the liquid in the pan as gravy.

FIREMAN'S SUPPER — "NANTUCKET"

This substantial dish is one that Nantucket firemen delighted in cooking for themselves one night a week.

Trim pork chops. Put a little fat into an iron

spider and fry the chops slowly on both sides.   Cover the upper side of the chops thickly with sliced onions.   Pare, slice, and add half a dozen potatoes. Season well with salt and pepper.   Cover all with cold water.   Simmer until potatoes are soft — about half an hour.   Keep closely covered.   Use the oven or the top of the stove as preferred.   Slow simmering is necessary in order to bring out the juices.

POT ROAST — "HYANNIS"

4 or 5 pounds beef	1 cup carrots, diced
2 tablespoons lard	2 peeled onions
3 cups warm water	½ cup prepared turnips
1 onion, diced	1 cup tomatoes

Flour, salt, pepper

The under part of the round is the best cut for this dish.   Rub the lard into the meat.   Dredge it with flour, salt, and pepper.   Sear on both sides in an iron kettle.   Add the warm water, diced onion, a bay leaf, and simmer several hours, closely covered. One hour before taking up, add to the kettle the carrots, onions, turnips, and tomatoes. Potatoes should be added, after peeling, half an hour before serving.   When tender, remove meat to a hot platter.   Thicken the gravy with a little flour. Cut the meat into slices and pour the brown gravy over it.   Arrange the vegetables around the edge of the platter.

TRIPE WITH ONIONS — "BREWSTER"

2 pounds fresh honeycomb tripe 2 onions
2 tablespoons butter 1 teaspoon sugar
1 minced carrot Salt, pepper

Wash tripe in cold water and cut into two-inch strips. Melt butter in a saucepan and fry the tripe lightly. Remove to a hot, buttered casserole. Fry the sliced onions in the melted butter. Add to the casserole. Put in the carrot, sugar, salt, and pepper. Cover with water. Simmer slowly one and a half hours, closely covered. Thicken the liquid with a little flour. Add a teaspoon of Worcestershire Sauce for extra flavoring. Serve in the casserole.

FRIED TRIPE, WITH SPANISH SAUCE

Wash the tripe, drain and cut into pieces of a size for serving. Boil twenty or thirty minutes or until very soft. Drain and dry with a cloth. Dip the pieces in beaten egg; dust with powdered cracker crumbs, and fry quickly in a hot spider, in butter. Serve with a Spanish or Horse-radish sauce. (See "Sauces.")

BAKED VEAL CUTLETS, WITH MUSHROOM SAUCE

Order rib chops, an inch thick. Place in a hot saucepan with a tablespoon of oil or butter and cook until evenly browned on both sides. Dredge with salt and pepper. Add to the pan half a cup stock or water and one teaspoon Worcestershire Sauce. Cover and bake in slow oven forty minutes. Remove cutlets. Strain the liquid and use in making a mushroom sauce. Place mashed potato or spinach in the middle of a round chop dish, and arrange the cutlets in a circle around the vegetable. Pour the sauce over the meat.

CHICKEN RICE PUDDING

2½ cups cooked chopped chicken
¾ cup chicken gravy
1½ cups uncooked rice
4 eggs beaten light
1 tablespoon butter
Salt, pepper, mace

Boil the rice until soft. Mix with the butter, beaten eggs, and mace. Butter a baking dish and line with the rice. Mix the chicken and gravy and pour into the middle. Season well. Cover top with the remaining rice. Bake thirty-five minutes in a hot oven. Unmold carefully on a hot platter. Pour around a cheese or curry sauce. Or make a circle of broiled tomatoes and serve the sauce separately.

IRISH STEW AND DUMPLINGS

2 pounds lamb or mutton
5 or 6 onions
4 small carrots
1 small turnip
4 potatoes diced
1 teaspoon salt
3 tablespoons flour

Order a piece of meat about two inches thick cut from the breast or shoulder. Trim off the fat and try it out. Cut the meat into pieces and brown it in the hot fat. Remove bits of fat and place the meat in a kettle, cover with boiling water, and simmer two hours, or until tender. Cut the carrots and turnip into pieces, use the onions whole, and put into kettle during the last hour of cooking, with the salt. Parboil the diced potatoes and add during the last fifteen minutes. Thicken the gravy with flour stirred into a little cold water. Serve with dumplings on a large platter.

DUMPLINGS FOR STEW

1½ cups flour
3 teaspoons baking powder
½ teaspoon salt
1 teaspoon butter
½ cup milk or water

Sift together the flour, salt, and baking powder, and work in the butter with the finger tips. Mix to a dough with the milk or water, cutting it in gradually with a knife. Roll out and cut with a biscuit cutter or drop from a spoon upon the boiling stew. Cover closely. Cook twelve or fifteen minutes. Extra dumplings may be placed on a perforated buttered tin and put into a covered steamer to cook.

GAME

WILD DUCK — " BARNSTABLE "

Prepare the ducks and wash thoroughly. Rub with salt and pepper and dredge with flour. Do not stuff but place an onion with several slices of apple and celery inside before baking. Put into a hot oven or at 450° F. and roast only about twenty-five minutes. Wild duck should be served rare. Serve with Bread Sauce and currant jelly.

ROASTED TEAL DUCKS

Remove the tiny pin feathers from the ducks and singe. Wash quickly in cold water inside and out. Wipe dry. Stuff, sew up, and place ducks on a rack in a baking pan. Cover with strips of fat salt pork. Dredge with flour, salt, and pepper. Have the oven very hot for the first five minutes, then cool a little. Add water to the pan and baste from time to time. Toward the end of cooking, remove the pork and allow the ducks to brown.

Dressing

1 cup bread crumbs	1 cup sour apples, chopped
1 cup boiled onions, chopped	Salt, pepper, and melted butter

POTTED PIGEONS

These are usually preferred stewed. Prepare the pigeons and tie up. Place them, breasts up, in a cooking pan and lay slices of bacon over them. Cut one carrot and one small onion into dice. Mix with one teaspoon chopped parsley, and one teaspoon salt. Sprinkle this mixture over the pigeons. Cover with water and simmer until the birds are tender, keeping pan tightly closed. Add more water if necessary. Remove the pigeons and thicken the liquid for gravy. Serve on thin slices of toast.

ROAST QUAIL ON TOAST

Cut the birds into halves. Roll in flour, salt, and pepper. Place slices of fat salt pork over the tops. Bake in a greased pan with a half cup of water. Add more water if needed. Baste with the liquid. When tender, remove the quails. Add rich milk to the drippings in the pan to make a gravy. Place the quails on toast and pour the gravy over them. If necessary, thicken the gravy with a little flour and brown with Kitchen Bouquet.

BROILED SQUABS

Split the squabs down the back. Spread out flat and brush both sides with melted butter or oil. Place on a hot greased broiler, flesh side toward heat.

Broil young squabs about twelve minutes. Melt two tablespoons butter for each bird and season with salt and pepper. Dip the squabs into this before placing them on buttered toast. Currant jell and watercress are good accompaniments.

ROASTED SQUABS

Dress and truss like young chickens. Skewer the legs close to the body. Rub all over with salt and pepper. Fasten a slice of salt pork across each breast. Bake fifteen to twenty minutes in hot oven or at 450° F. basting with melted butter. Serve on buttered toast and pour the pan liquor over.

VEGETABLES

APPLE FRITTERS

2 tart apples	1 egg well beaten
1⅓ cups flour	⅔ cup milk
1 teaspoon baking powder	¼ teaspoon salt

Sift together dry ingredients. Beat the egg and mix with milk. Combine all into a creamy batter. Pare and core the apples. Cut them into slices. Mix with the batter, covering well, and drop from a spoon into deep hot fat, heated to 365° F.

APPLE RINGS

Core, do not peel, the apples. Cut into slices about one inch thick. Make a syrup by boiling half a cup sugar with half a cup water. When thickened, drop in the rings. They become soft quickly. Serve with meat dishes.

APPLE SAUCE

Peel and core three cups of apples. Cut them into eighths and stew with a quarter cup water and a half cup sugar. Add gratings of nutmeg and cinnamon. The sauce is sometimes put through a purée strainer but has a better flavor when served plain.   A few bits of butter may be added while the sauce is hot.

GRIDDLED APPLES

Choose large tart apples.   Peel and core them, and cut into one-inch slices.   Butter a griddle generously and brown the apples first one side, then the other.

ASPARAGUS TIPS

These may be freshly cut from the stalks or canned. If canned, drain from their juice and cook with two tablespoons butter until thoroughly hot.   Serve with an egg sauce on slices of toast.   If fresh tips are used, cook fifteen minutes in boiling salted water.   If served hot, use Hollandaise Sauce.   If cold, a Vinaigrette Sauce is very nice.   (See "Sauces.")

BAKED BANANAS

2 tablespoons butter	2 tablespoons lemon juice
3 tablespoons sugar	Slightly underripe bananas

Peel bananas and lay whole, or cut once lengthwise, in a buttered pan.   Pour the mixture over them and bake until tender, basting often.   Use remainder of sauce to pour over when served.

BANANA FRITTERS

½ cup milk	1 teaspoon sugar
½ cup flour	1 teaspoon butter
1 teaspoon baking powder	Yolk 1 egg
Pinch of salt	

Mix ingredients well together. Cut bananas lengthwise then across once. Cover each piece with the batter and fry in hot fat until golden brown. Serve with Lemon or Orange Sauce.

"SNUG HAVEN" BAKED BEANS

1 pint "California" pea beans	3 teaspoons salt
½ pound fat salt pork	3 tablespoons sugar
½ cup dark molasses	2 teaspoons dry mustard
2 cups boiling water	

Wash in several waters and discard all imperfect beans. Soak overnight in water to cover. In the morning drain them, and parboil for one and a half hours. Scald the pork and bury it deep in a New England bean pot and cover with the parboiled beans, which have been drained in a colander with cold water poured through. Mix molasses, mustard, salt, and sugar. Add boiling water. Pour the mixture over the beans and pork. Add water to cover them. Cover bean pot. Place in moderate oven and bake from six to seven hours. Once in two hours look at the beans to see if more water is necessary. Toward last of cooking, the water should be well absorbed and the beans dark, rich, and delectable.

BAKED BEETS

Young beets are especially good baked instead of boiled in the usual fashion. Leave on an inch or so of the tops when washing and trimming them as in this way the color is preserved. Place them in a baking pan with a little water to prevent burning and bake until tender.

PICKLED BEETS

Boil the beets until tender, leaving on an inch of the tops. Drain. When cool remove skin and tops, and slice. Heat three cups vinegar with two thirds cup of sugar and one teaspoon salt. Stir until dissolved. Then pour while hot over the sliced beets. Set aside to become cool before using.

BROCCOLI — BOILED

Soak the broccoli in cold salted water for half an hour to remove sand, etc. Drain and trim stalks to an even length. Add salt to a kettle of boiling water. Tie the broccoli in a cheesecloth in order to facilitate removing and boil twenty-five minutes. Serve plain with butter or on toast like asparagus with Hollandaise or Drawn Butter Sauce.

BROCCOLI — VINAIGRETTE

Boil broccoli carefully as above. Let cool. Pour over a Vinaigrette Sauce and serve on individual plates.

CARROTS, BAKED "LOG CABIN"

Scrape and boil or steam whole young carrots until tender. Season with salt and pepper. Pile them, log-cabin fashion, in a baking dish. Lay several thin slices of bacon over the top and bake until the bacon is crisp. The oven should be hot or at 400° F.

GLAZED CARROTS

Cut scraped carrots into balls or fancy shapes with a small vegetable cutter. Cover with a minimum amount of boiling salted water and cook until tender. Keeping the dish covered helps to retain the flavor. Melt in a saucepan two or three tablespoons of butter with an equal amount of sugar. Toss the carrots about in this hot mixture until they are glazed and slightly brown. A tablespoon of finely minced mint leaves may be added for variation.

FRIED CARROTS

Cut tender cooked carrots into halves or quarters. Dip the pieces in milk and roll in flour until coated all over. Place in a frying basket and dip into hot fat heated to 375° F. until delicately browned. Drain on paper. Season with salt and a bit of sugar. Serve hot.

CAULIFLOWER AND CHEESE

1 head of cauliflower	1 cup milk
2 tablespoons butter	4 tablespoons grated cheese
1½ tablespoons flour	3 tablespoons dry bread crumbs

Boil cauliflower in salted water until tender. Drain. Cut apart the flowerettes. Make a white sauce of butter, flour, and milk.   Place layers of the cauliflower in a buttered baking dish.   Season with salt and pepper, and sprinkle with cheese.   Repeat until all is used.   Pour the white sauce over all. Sprinkle more cheese and the bread crumbs over the top.   Bake about fifteen minutes or until brown.

BRAISED CELERY

Two or more full bunches of celery.   Clean.   Remove fiber.   Scrape the roots but do not remove. Cut off the leaves to dry as seasoning.   Split the stalks lengthwise.   Soak in cold water to remove sand.   Tie lengths together to resemble original bunch.   Parboil a few minutes in boiling water. Drain.   In a covered baking dish or casserole arrange several slices of bacon or salt pork, with two slices each of onions and carrots.   Place the celery on them and cover with water in which vegetables have been boiled, or other stock well seasoned.   Bake until tender.   Remove celery and keep hot while making a sauce of the liquid thickened with flour and a teaspoon of cooking sherry for flavoring.   Pour this over the celery and serve very hot.

CREAMED CELERY AND GREEN PEPPERS

1½ cups crisp celery	3 tablespoons flour
1 green pepper	3 tablespoons butter
1½ cups milk	Salt, pepper

Slices of toast

Cut the celery into inch pieces and boil in slightly salted water. Core and seed the pepper and cut it into slices. Make a white sauce of butter, flour, and milk. Drain the celery when tender. Mix together the pepper, celery, and white sauce, when thick and smooth. Season as needed and serve on toast.

GREEN CORN FRITTERS NUMBER I

2 cups corn pulp	½ cup milk
2 eggs beaten	Flour to make batter
	Salt, pepper

Score the kernels on the cob down the middle with a sharp knife and press out the pulp, using the dull back of the knife. Make a batter of the remaining ingredients, adding flour in small quantities until the right consistency is obtained. Mix with the pulp. Grease and heat a griddle. Drop the batter from a spoon in small cakes. Brown both sides. Canned corn may be used if drained well.

CORN FRITTERS NUMBER II

2 or 3 ears of corn	1 egg beaten
¾ cup flour	2 tablespoons minced parsley
1 teaspoon baking powder	Salt, pepper

Scrape the kernels from the ears. Sift flour, baking powder, and salt. Add the egg, seasonings, and corn. Beat thoroughly. Drop from a spoon on a hot greased griddle or into deep hot fat. If the corn is not juicy, add a tablespoon of milk.

NANTUCKET CORN PUDDING

2 cups corn	1 teaspoon salt
2 eggs slightly beaten	1 teaspoon sugar
2 cups milk	⅛ teaspoon pepper

Scrape the corn from the ear and mix with remaining ingredients. Canned corn may be used but should be run through the food chopper before mixing. Bake slowly in a buttered baking dish, like custard. Serve as a vegetable with meat or fish.

CORN, CHEESE, AND SPAGHETTI

1 can sweet corn	1 tablespoon flour
¼ cup grated cheese	1 tablespoon butter
½ package spaghetti, boiled	1 can condensed tomato soup

Make a paste of the flour, butter, and tomato soup. Add the cheese and stir well. Put in the drained corn and the cooked spaghetti. Bake in a buttered dish uncovered. This is a substantial luncheon dish.

ROASTED GREEN CORN

Do not remove the husks from the corn but place in a slow oven and bake half an hour. Then take off the husks and silk fringe and serve hot with butter. This has the flavor of the roasted corn served at clambakes.

BAKED CUCUMBERS

Choose large cucumbers. Split them lengthwise. Remove pulp and chop it with one teaspoon onion, half a tomato, half a green pepper, and seasoning of salt and pepper. Chop all fine. Add one tablespoon buttered bread crumbs, and one teaspoon melted butter to mix. Fill the cavities of the cucumbers, making a little heap nicely rounded. Bake one hour in a moderate oven or at 350° F. Serve with a butter sauce.

FRIED CUCUMBERS

Pare the cucumbers. Cut them into several slices lengthwise. Dry well. Sprinkle with salt and pepper. Roll in fine crumbs, beaten egg, and crumbs again. Fry in deep fat and drain on brown paper.

BAKED EGGPLANT

1 small eggplant	2 tablespoons butter
1 onion, chopped	½ cup boiling water
1 cup soft bread crumbs	1 teaspoon salt

Peel and slice the eggplant. Cut into cubes. Lay them for half an hour in cold, salted water. Drain. Mix together the crumbs, onion, and seasonings. Place with the eggplant in a greased baking dish. Pour over the boiling water and the butter in bits. Bake in moderate oven, or at 350° F., for one hour or until tender.

FRIED EGGPLANT

Wash but do not peel an eggplant. Cut into slices crosswise. Beat an egg slightly. Prepare finely rolled cracker crumbs. Season the sliced plant with salt and pepper. Roll in flour, egg, and cracker crumbs. Fry in deep fat at 350° F. until brown. Good with Tartar Sauce.

EGGPLANT AND OYSTER PIE

½ cup oysters cut into pieces   ½ cup milk
3 cups eggplant cubes   1 tablespoon butter
½ cup cracker crumbs   Salt, pepper
Biscuit dough

Boil the eggplant cubes fifteen minutes. Drain. Make a biscuit dough and divide for top and under crust of a greased baking dish. Melt the butter and mix with cracker crumbs. Add the oysters and combine all ingredients. Bake as a pie, perforating the top crust, for forty-five minutes in a moderate oven, or at 400° F.

LIMA BEAN LOAF

2 cups cooked Lima beans   1 egg beaten
1 cup soft bread crumbs   2 tablespoons minced onion
½ cup chopped green   2 tablespoons tomato catsup
  peppers   ½ cup cooked carrots or peas

Use either fresh or canned beans. Mix together all ingredients, seasoning well with salt and pepper, and mashing the beans. Turn into a small buttered bread pan. Bake in moderate oven about twenty-five minutes. Horseradish or Tomato Sauce should be served with it.

MUSHROOMS ON TOAST

Remove the stalks and peel the mushrooms. Place them, dark side down, in a dish of cold salted water to remove dirt or insects. Dry them carefully. Place two tablespoons of butter in a saucepan. Add the mushrooms, dark side down and simmer eight minutes. Turn them over and continue cooking ten minutes more. Season with salt and pepper and serve on toast.

MUSHROOMS BAKED UNDER GLASS

The small glass oven "bells" are necessary for this delicious way of cooking mushrooms. Choose large, fine mushrooms. Peel and remove stems. Reserve one of the largest mushrooms for each service. Cut up the others with the stems. Sauté in butter, until light brown, rounds of bread cut to fit under the bells. Place a large mushroom, cup side up, on each round. Fill the cups with chopped mushrooms. Season with salt, pepper, and bits of butter. Pour on two tablespoons of cream for each mushroom and put on the bell covers. Bake in a hot oven fifteen minutes. Do not remove the bell but serve as taken from the oven.

GLAZED ONIONS

Choose small white onions.   Cook them in slightly salted boiling water about twenty minutes, until tender but not too well done.   Remove from water and place in a saucepan with two tablespoons melted butter.   Roll the onions about in the butter, sprinkling them with a little powdered sugar.   Turn often to brown them evenly.   As the butter is absorbed, add a tablespoon of the hot water in which the onions were cooked, and more when necessary.   Season with pepper and salt.

CREAMED ONIONS

Boil the onions in slightly salted water until tender, but remove while still shapely.   Save the onion water.   Make a white sauce with half milk and half onion water.   Pour this over the freshly boiled onions.

FRENCH FRIED POTATOES

Pare white potatoes of uniform size.   Cut them lengthwise into eighths.   Soak an hour in cold water. Dry thoroughly with a cloth.   Place a layer in a frying basket and immerse in hot fat at 360° F. until golden brown.   Drain on brown paper and sprinkle with salt.   Repeat until all are fried.   It is important to dip only a few at a time, as too many will not brown evenly.   To make them crisp, dip them a

second time into the fat at an increased temperature.
Drain and sprinkle with salt as before.

POTATO AND CHEESE CROQUETTES

2 cups cold mashed potato   1 tablespoon grated cheese
1 egg yolk beaten   1 tablespoon milk
Salt, pepper, onion extract

Mix in order given. Shape into croquettes.
Brush over with crumbs, egg, and crumbs. Fry in
deep fat, at 390° F.

CANDIED SWEET POTATOES

Pare sweet potatoes. Boil them ten minutes.
Cut into slices lengthwise. Butter a baking dish.
Put in a layer of potatoes. Sprinkle generously with
brown sugar, bits of butter and salt to taste. Then
add more potatoes and repeat until dish is filled.
Pour over half a cup of hot water and cover the dish.
Bake about three quarters of an hour. Uncover to
brown. Baste with melted butter and sugar after
the first twenty minutes.

GRIDDLED SWEET POTATOES

Slice cold boiled sweet potatoes lengthwise. Butter a griddle. When hot, brown the potatoes first
one side then the other. Sprinkle with a little salt.
Serve hot.

SWEET POTATO SOUFFLÉ

6 boiled sweet potatoes	2 eggs, separated
2 tablespoons butter	1 teaspoon salt

Mash the potatoes while hot.   Mix with the butter
and salt.   Let stand until cooled.   Beat the egg
yolks and stir in.   Whip the whites stiff and fold in.
Butter a baking dish just large enough for the mixture and heap it in lightly.   Brown in a quick oven,
or at 325° F.

SWEET POTATO CROQUETTES

2 cups mashed sweet potatoes	1 egg
1 teaspoon butter	Salt, pepper

Season the potato with salt, pepper, and butter.
Beat in the egg thoroughly.   Shape in cylinder form;
roll in powdered cracker crumbs, beaten egg, crumbs,
and fry in deep fat at 390° F.

SWEET POTATO AND APPLE CASSEROLE

4 or 5 sweet potatoes boiled	2 teaspoons salt
4 large apples	3 tablespoons butter
½ cup brown sugar	½ cup hot water

Pare and slice the potatoes.   Core, pare, and slice
the apples.   Butter a casserole and arrange the
apples and potatoes in alternate layers.   Cover each
layer with sugar, salt, and bits of butter.   Add the
hot water.   Cover closely and bake until apples are
tender and the top browned.   Hot oven or at 400° F.

BAKED SQUASH

Squash when baked has a flavor never attainable by boiling or steaming. A Hubbard squash is best. Wash and split it into several large pieces. Remove the seeds. Sprinkle on salt, pepper, and a little melted butter. Place in a moderate oven, skin side down, and bake until tender. It may be served in the shell, in which case the pieces should be more carefully cut into squares or triangles before baking. Or if preferred, remove the yellow pulp; mash it in a bowl with two tablespoons butter and one tablespoon of cream. Add salt to taste.

PILGRIM SUCCOTASH

2 cups cooked beans, (Lima or kidney)	1 teaspoon salt
	2 tablespoons butter
2 cups cooked corn, cut from cob	1 teaspoon sugar
	¼ cup milk

Melt the butter. Add the beans and corn with a little water and the seasonings. Stir in the milk as water is absorbed. Heat thoroughly but do not boil after milk is added. Serve very hot.

MASHED TURNIPS

Wash and peel two good-sized turnips. Cut them into quarters. Cook in boiling slightly salted water about three quarters of an hour or until tender. Drain well, pressing out all the water. Mash and beat smooth with two tablespoons butter and a teaspoon of salt.   Sprinkle on a little pepper after the turnip is arranged in serving dish.

TURNIP CUPS

Boil turnips of even size as for mashed turnips, adding a little sugar in the cooking water with the salt.   When tender, cut rounds from the centers about two inches thick.   Make a little hollow in the top and fill with creamed carrots, peas, or vegetable combinations.   Season well and serve with the meat course.

ESCALLOPED TOMATOES

1 can tomatoes or 3 cups fresh tomatoes	1 teaspoon minced onion
	1 teaspoon salt
2 cups fine bread crumbs	1 tablespoon sugar
2 tablespoons melted butter	

Drain the canned tomatoes or peel and chop the fresh ones.   Place a layer at bottom of a buttered baking dish.   Sprinkle on sugar and melted butter. Add a layer of crumbs and seasonings, including the onion.   When dish is full, have crumbs at the top with melted butter over them.   Bake about half an hour in moderate oven, or at 350° F.

GRILLED TOMATOES

Choose tomatoes not fully ripe.   Cut them into slices, unpeeled.   Spread out on a platter a mixture of two tablespoons flour, one teaspoon salt, and a little pepper. Drop the tomato slices in this, coating both sides. Broil quickly on a greased broiler. Serve with fish or meat course.

STUFFED GREEN PEPPERS

Slice off the stem end and remove cores and fiber. Stuff with a mixture made of one cup fine bread crumbs, one chopped tomato, one teaspoon minced onion, one teaspoon salt, a speck of pepper, and two tablespoons melted butter. Place the peppers in a buttered pan with a cup of hot water and bake half an hour while basting with the liquid in the pan. Many other fillings are possible:

Creamed potatoes, sprinkled over with buttered bread crumbs.

Boiled rice mixed with a highly seasoned tomato sauce.

Canned corn mixed with minced green pepper.

Small oysters as given under Fish dishes.

CREAMED POTATOES

Cut boiled potatoes into dice. Melt two tablespoons of butter in a saucepan. Toss the diced potatoes in this until coated. Season with salt and pepper and a little minced parsley. Mix a tablespoon of flour with a cup of cold milk and stir in. Heat all thoroughly together until the milk is thickened and serve.

DUCHESS POTATOES

2 cups hot potatoes, riced	2 egg yolks
2 tablespoons butter	Salt, pepper
Milk	

Beat all the ingredients together until light.   Use
a little milk if needed to make the mixture right for a
pastry bag.   Force it through into little rosettes or
other shapes.   Brush over with the beaten white of
egg diluted with milk and brown in a hot oven.
These potatoes are used with planked dishes.

HASHED BROWN POTATOES

Heat two tablespoons bacon fat or other drippings
in a saucepan.   Cut cold cooked potatoes into dice
and add.   Cover with cold milk.   As the milk begins
to simmer, hash the potatoes fine with a knife.   Season with salt and pepper.   Keep turning over the
potatoes with the knife while cooking.   When the
milk is absorbed, press down as flat as possible on the
bottom of the pan and allow to brown.   When an
even brown crust has formed, fold over like an omelet
and serve with a garnish of parsley.

STUFFED BAKED POTATOES

Bake large potatoes.   Cut a slice from one side of
each and scoop out the potato carefully.   Mash with
sweet cream, salt, and a teaspoon of grated cheese

for each potato. Beat together until light. Fill the skins but do not pack down. Sprinkle more cheese over the tops. Set into the oven to brown. The hard beating makes them puff up above the shells.

POTATO CRUST

For any kind of meat pies

4 cups boiled mashed potatoes	2 teaspoons baking powder
2 tablespoons shortening	1 egg well beaten
2 teaspoons salt	6 tablespoons milk
1 teaspoon grated onion	Paprika

Beat all well together. Spread one inch thick on top of meat pies. Brush over with milk. Bake about an hour in moderate oven.

STUFFED BAKED TOMATOES

6 firm red tomatoes	1 cup bread crumbs
1 cup cooked meat	Melted butter
½ onion minced	Salt, pepper

Wash but do not peel the tomatoes. Slice off the stem ends and scoop out the inside with a sharp knife. Chop meat fine, and mix with the tomato pulp, bread crumbs, and seasonings. Use melted butter to moisten. Stuff the tomatoes carefully. Place them on a greased baking pan to bake about half an hour. The oven must not be hot enough to cause the tomatoes to burst their skins. 350° F. is a good temperature.

VEGETABLE HASH

2 cups boiled potatoes
1 cup boiled beets
1 cup boiled carrots
½ cup cooked turnips
1 slice fat salt pork

The vegetables may be those remaining from a boiled dinner or they may be cooked especially. Many other combinations are equally good; in such case, twice the bulk of potatoes is a good proportion. Cut the pork into bits and try out. Turn in the finely chopped vegetables. Sprinkle them with salt and pepper, and if dry, moisten with a half cup of hot stock or boiling water. Smooth the hash down to fit the pan. Cover and let cook. When the fat is absorbed, let the hash brown on the bottom. Then fold over like an omelet. It is sometimes liked with a poached egg on top, or one for each service.

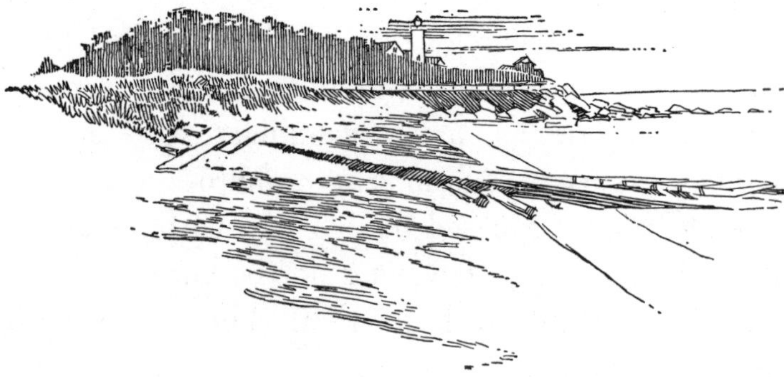

SALADS

APPLE AND CABBAGE SALAD

⅔ cup shredded cabbage   1½ cups apples, diced
Lettuce leaves for cups

Crisp the cabbage for an hour or more in ice-cold water. Dice the apples just before mixing. Use Boiled Salad Dressing. Take care to dry the cabbage thoroughly before mixing.

ARTICHOKE BOTTOMS

The artichoke bottoms put up in jars make most convenient and delicious salads. Rinse in cold water when taken from the jar. Drain and spread with mayonnaise and a macedoine of cooked vegetables — string beans, minced carrots, cauliflower, peas, or various combinations of cold vegetables at hand. Serve very cold with a spoonful of mayonnaise on top.

ASPARAGUS TIPS JELLIED

Use small deep cups or molds. Prepare the tips by cutting to a size to line the molds, tips down. Make a plain or tomato jelly, and keep in liquid state over hot water. Pour a little into each cup and spread it over the sides to form a coating.   When firm, place the asparagus tips around the sides of the molds. Fill molds with the liquid jelly and set aside to grow firm.   Unmold on lettuce and serve mayonnaise or use it as a garnish around the salad.

BANANA NUT SALAD

Remove tips and strings from ripe bananas.   Cut each one into three pieces.   Put through a grinder walnut or pecan meats.   Roll the bananas in the nut meats.   Place on lettuce leaves.   Cover with Fruit or Whipped Cream Dressing.   Add a few pieces of marshmallows if liked.

CARROT AND BANANA SALAD

3 bananas   ¼ cup salted peanuts
2 small carrots uncooked

Dice the bananas.   Run carrots and peanuts through the food chopper.   Mix with bananas.   Add salad dressing to moisten and serve in lettuce cups.

CELERY STUFFED

Crisp the celery stalks.   Do not remove the young tender leaves.   Make a stuffing of equal parts of Roquefort and cream cheese.   Beat them together and moisten with either French salad dressing or mayonnaise.   Fill the grooves of the stalks with the mixture and set aside to chill. A pastry bag with plain tube is the best means of filling the grooves.

CELERY AND PECAN SALAD

1½ cups celery, diced
¾ cup pecan meats, broken

1 cup white cabbage, shredded
Lettuce

Mix at last moment before serving with Cream or Boiled Dressing. Serve in crisp lettuce cups.

COLE SLAW

Shred a firm white cabbage and place in ice water for an hour. When needed, drain thoroughly and mix with dressing.

Dressing

1 egg
2 tablespoons sugar
1 tablespoon flour

1 tablespoon vinegar
1 cup milk
Pinch of salt

1 heaping teaspoon mustard

Beat the egg well. Mix with other ingredients in order given. Cook in double boiler until it thickens. Set aside to cool.

CUCUMBER JELLY SALAD

4 large or 5 small cucumbers
2 tablespoons gelatine

4 cups water
1 slice of onion

1 teaspoon salt

After peeling and cutting the green ends from the cucumbers, slice them and stew in four cups of water until soft, having a slice of onion, salt, and pepper in the cooking water. Soak the gelatine in water to cover and stir into the hot mixture. Strain and pour into individual molds or use a large ring mold if preferred. A few slices of the cucumber may be reserved to place in the molds before the gelatine is poured over. A ring mold may be filled with cold salmon-mayonnaise, or diced celery. The individual molds should be served on lettuce with a mayonnaise dressing.

STUFFED EGG SALAD

6 hard-boiled eggs
1 teaspoon minced parsley
½ teaspoon olive oil
Onion and lemon juice
Crisp lettuce leaves

Shell the eggs and cut into halves lengthwise. Rub the yolks through a sieve and add the oil and seasonings. Mix well. Fill the whites with the mixture and set to chill. Place two stuffed halves on lettuce cups. French dressing made with Tarragon vinegar is appropriate for this salad, using it with the lettuce leaves.

FISH SALAD IN ASPIC

2 cups cold boiled fish
¾ cup hot fish stock or consommé
1 tablespoon gelatine
¼ cup cold water
¾ cup chilled whipped cream
Salt, lemon juice

Salmon or halibut flaked are especially good as salad. Soak the gelatine fifteen minutes in the cold water. Dissolve in the hot stock. Strain. Set the dish over cracked ice. Whip hard as it begins to thicken and beat in the stiffly whipped cream and the flaked fish. Season as needed with lemon juice, salt, etc. A large ring mold is very pretty for this salad. Wet it inside and fill. Turn out when very cold on a bed of lettuce with mayonnaise dressing. Sliced cucumbers are very good with it, arranged in a circle about the molds.

FRUIT SALAD

4 navel oranges	2 bananas
2 grapefruit	2 slices canned pineapple

Cut the fruit, after peeling, into cubes or dice, and chill. Mix with Fruit Salad Dressing or a French dressing made with lemon juice. A half cup of broken nut meats is sometimes added. Serve on crisp lettuce leaves.

JELLIED FRUIT SALAD

2 tablespoons gelatine	½ cup white cherries, stoned
4 tablespoons cold water	½ cup red cherries, stoned
½ cup boiling water	½ cup sliced peaches
4 tablespoons lemon juice	1 cup diced pineapple
2 tablespoons sugar	

Soak gelatine five minutes in cold water. Dissolve in the boiling water and stir until clear. Add lemon

juice and sugar. Mix and set to cool. When partly
cold add the fruit and pour into a wet ring mold.
Let it stiffen and chill. When wanted to use, unmold carefully on crisp lettuce and fill center with
Fruit Salad Dressing mixed with whipped cream.

FROZEN TOMATO SALAD

1 can tomato *or*	1 teaspoon mild vinegar
6 or 8 fresh tomatoes	1½ teaspoons gelatine
2 onions quartered	1½ cups cream
2 tablespoons sugar	Salt, paprika

Cook together the tomatoes with the onions and
seasonings until very soft. Press through a sieve to
obtain as much pulp as possible. Let cool. Soak
gelatine in cold water to cover. Dissolve over hot
water. Mix with the tomato, beat all together
thoroughly. Whip the cream and mix. Turn into
a mold and bury in ice several hours. Garnish when
unmolded with cucumber slices or hard-boiled eggs.

GELATINE BASE FOR VEGETABLE SALADS

2 tablespoons gelatine	2 tablespoons sugar
½ cup mild vinegar	½ teaspoon salt
2 cups boiling water	½ teaspoon lemon juice

Soak the gelatine five minutes in cold water to
cover. Add the boiling water to dissolve, and the
remaining ingredients. When beginning to thicken
add two cups of any cooked vegetable or a macedoine of vegetables. Pour into a mold or individual
timbale molds and chill.

HALIBUT AND CELERY SALAD

2 cups boiled halibut, flaked

1 cup celery, diced

½ cup cooked cauliflower pieces

¼ teaspoon minced onion

Chill the ingredients before mixing. Combine at the last moment before serving with Vinaigrette Sauce or Mayonnaise. Serve in lettuce cups.

JELLIED MINT SALAD

¾ cup fresh mint, minced

2 tablespoons gelatine

2 cups boiling water

1 teaspoon lemon juice

½ cup vinegar

½ teaspoon salt

2 rounded tablespoons sugar

Green coloring

Soak the gelatine five minutes in cold water to cover. Dissolve in boiling water with the seasonings added. Do not allow to cool but stir in the finely cut mint and keep the mixture liquid over hot water for twenty minutes to extract the mint flavor. Add a little coloring matter. Strain and set to stiffen and chill. When firm, cut into cubes and serve with cucumber or tomato salad or with cold meats.

JELLIED VEGETABLE MAYONNAISE SALAD

1½ cups cooked vegetables, diced

French dressing to cover

1 cup jellied mayonnaise

Many combinations are possible for this salad,— string beans, cauliflower, carrots, turnips, Brussels sprouts, etc. Canned ones may be used if drained and rinsed in cold water and well dried with a cloth before mixing. Cut the vegetables into dice and marinate in French dressing half an hour or so. Drain and stir gently into the jellied mayonnaise before it grows firm. Fill small cups or timbale molds with the mixture and invert when chilled, on crisp lettuce leaves.

ORANGE SALAD

This is an especially good salad to serve with game. Choose rather sour oranges, one for each service. Peel. Discard the ends and remove seeds. Slice quarter of an inch thick. Place the slices overlapping in a circle on crisp lettuce. Use a French dressing made with lemon juice.

POTATO SALAD

2 cups cold boiled potatoes	2 tablespoons green peppers
2 hard-boiled eggs	2 tablespoons sweet pickle

1 cup celery

Cut the potato into cubes. Chop the peppers and pickle. Cut the eggs into large pieces. Dice the celery. Keep all very cold. Mix with boiled salad dressing just before using. A little minced parsley may be added if liked.

RED PEPPER AND CAULIFLOWER SALAD

Select large sweet red peppers. Slice off the tops and remove seeds. Marinate pieces of cold boiled cauliflower in French dressing. Fill the pepper shells. Grate raw carrot over the top. Serve with mayonnaise on pale green lettuce leaves. This is colorful and appetizing.

SALMON MOLDS

2 cups cold salmon, canned or fresh	1½ teaspoons salt
1 tablespoon gelatine	1 tablespoon sugar
¼ cup cold water	4 tablespoons lemon juice
2 egg yolks	1 tablespoon butter
½ teaspoon flour	¾ cup milk
	1 teaspoon ground mustard

Soak gelatine in cold water. Beat egg yolks until lemon colored. Mix together the flour, salt, sugar, and mustard. Stir in the egg yolks, lemon juice, and milk. Place dish over hot water and stir constantly until thickened. Take from fire and add the butter and gelatine. When well dissolved, stir in the flaked salmon. Chill in wet molds. Turn out on lettuce.

SHRIMP SALAD

1 cup shrimps, canned or fresh	1 tablespoon chopped pickles
1 cup diced celery *or* 1 cup cabbage, shredded	1 teaspoon salt
2 hard-boiled eggs, diced	⅔ cup mayonnaise

If shrimps are canned, rinse in cold water to freshen. Drain and dry. Mix with celery, eggs, and pickle. Season with salt and a little lemon juice. Arrange in lettuce cups on a platter. Place a spoonful of mayonnaise over each salad.

TOMATO JELLY SALAD

1 quart canned or chopped fresh tomatoes	1 sliced onion
	3 cloves
1½ cups boiling water	1 tablespoon vinegar
2 teaspoons sugar	1 teaspoon salt
2 tablespoons gelatine	

Combine tomatoes, water, and seasonings, including the vinegar. Simmer twenty minutes. Strain through a cheesecloth. There should be about three cups of juice. Soak gelatine five minutes in cold water and stir in. Place in a large dish to become firm. Serve plain, cut into squares, or use as a garnish. This jelly may be used as a base for cold mixed vegetables.

TOMATO SURPRISE SALAD

Choose firm red tomatoes, one for each service. Pour boiling water over them, peel quickly, and chill. Remove tops and as much of the pulp as possible. Fill with any of the following mixtures with a spoonful of mayonnaise on top:

Shrimps, celery, and green peppers.
Cold boiled asparagus and cauliflower.
Diced cucumbers, minced onion.
Hard-boiled eggs and endive, diced.
Potato salad and string beans.
Shredded cabbage, olives, and nuts, chopped.

WALDORF SALAD

1 cup tart apples, peeled and diced
½ cup chopped walnut meats
½ cup diced celery
½ cup mayonnaise
Chicory or lettuce leaves

Mix the cold ingredients together quickly. Place in little mounds on chicory or lettuce leaves which have been lightly dressed with French dressing. A spoonful of mayonnaise on top. The original salad was served in bright red apples, using the pulp for mixing.

SALAD DRESSINGS

BOILED SALAD DRESSING

2 cups milk	2 teaspoons mustard
2 tablespoons butter	2 teaspoons salt
8 tablespoons sugar	3 eggs, separated
4 tablespoons flour	¾ cup vinegar

Put into a double boiler all the ingredients, except the eggs and vinegar. Beat egg yolks and stir in. When thickened, add the vinegar and the whites of the eggs beaten well. Let cool. Add one pint of any good commercial mayonnaise. Beat all together hard, with an egg beater. This amount makes three pints.

CREAM SALAD DRESSING

1 heaping teaspoon each of mustard, salt, and sugar	½ cup vinegar
	1 tablespoon butter
2½ teaspoons flour	½ cup cream, sweet or sour
Yolks of 2 eggs	

Mix together the dry ingredients. Beat the egg yolks and add to the seasonings. Heat vinegar and butter. When hot, pour over the egg yolks. Place all together over hot water and stir until it thickens. When cool, add the cream, whipped.

FRENCH DRESSING

⅓ cup olive oil
2 tablespoons Tarragon vinegar

½ teaspoon salt
⅛ teaspoon paprika

Place the ingredients in a glass fruit jar. Screw on the top. Shake the contents until thoroughly mixed.

FRUIT SALAD DRESSING

Whip one cup of cream and mix with half cup mayonnaise for a delicious fruit salad dressing. When using a French dressing with fruits, mix it with lemon juice instead of vinegar.

HORSE-RADISH MAYONNAISE

Use the freshly grated horse-radish if it can be had. If the bottled is used, drain well before mixing. Combine two tablespoons of grated horse-radish with two cups of mayonnaise. Mix just before using. This is especially good with vegetable salads or cold meats.

JELLIED MAYONNAISE

1 teaspoon gelatine
2 tablespoons cold water

1 cup mayonnaise

Soak the gelatine in cold water five minutes. Let stand over hot water to dissolve. Beat it, while cooling, into the mayonnaise. Mix with any salad combination desired.

RELIABLE MAYONNAISE

1 large egg	1½ tablespoons vinegar
½ teaspoon salt	1½ tablespoons lemon juice
⅛ teaspoon paprika	1½ or 2 cups olive oil

Mix the egg, salt, and paprika in a cool bowl. Beat with rotary egg beater until well mixed. Add the lemon juice and vinegar. Put in, a teaspoonful at a time, the oil, beating after each addition. Then put it in by tablespoonfuls as the dressing begins to thicken, continuing until no more will be absorbed. When the dressing holds its shape, beat in a tablespoon of boiling water to bind it. Set to chill before using. Keep in covered jar.

WHIPPED CREAM DRESSING

3 egg yolks	½ teaspoon mustard
2 tablespoons sugar	½ cup hot vinegar
¼ teaspoon salt	2 teaspoons butter
½ cup cream	

Beat the yolks until light. Mix together the sugar, salt, and mustard and beat in. Heat the vinegar and butter. Put all together in a double boiler over hot water and stir until thickened. Let cool. Whip the cream and add when about to serve.

RUSSIAN DRESSING

Mix a few teaspoons of chili sauce and a quarter teaspoon onion juice with French dressing and beat well. Chill before using.

THOUSAND ISLAND DRESSING

1 cup mayonnaise
1 tablespoon chopped
  pimento

1 tablespoon minced green
  pepper
1 tablespoon chili sauce

Mix the savories together and stir into the mayonnaise. A little whipped cream may be added just before using.

TARRAGON VINEGAR

Scald a handful of fresh or dried tarragon leaves. Add two tablespoons brown sugar. Fill a wide-mouthed jar with the leaves and a quart of ordinary vinegar. Screw on the top and let stand two or more weeks until thoroughly seasoned. Then drain off the tarragon-flavored vinegar. Bottle and cork.

An herb garden, furnishing the seasonings most used in making salads, is a great convenience. If garden space is not available, grow the herbs in a window box. The French tarragon plants are perennials and very easily grown. Parsley must be sown early to allow plenty of time for its slow germinating. Chives, sage, mint, thyme, and sweet basil are all delightful seasonings and may be grown from seed for the planting.

CHEESE

CHEESE BALLS

3 cups grated cheese	4 egg whites
2 tablespoons flour	⅛ teaspoon pepper
½ teaspoon salt	Cracker crumbs

Mix together the cheese, flour, salt, and pepper. Beat egg whites stiff and stir in. Shape into tiny balls. Roll in powdered cracker crumbs, egg, and crumbs again. Fry in deep fat at 385° F. until golden brown. Very nice with a salad course.

CRACKERS AND CHEESE

Use Boston crackers, split and toasted on the inside. Spread the toasted side with melted butter and a little paprika. Cover thickly with grated cheese. Set into the oven to cook a few minutes until the cheese is soft and creamy. Serve hot.

HOT CHEESE CROQUETTES

⅓ cup butter	2 eggs, yolks separated
⅓ cup flour	1½ cups cheese cut fine
1¼ cups milk	Pepper or paprika
⅓ teaspoon salt	Fine bread crumbs

Make a thick white sauce of butter, flour, seasonings, and milk.   Add the cheese and stir until melted.
Beat the egg yolks and stir in.   Do not cook after
the yolks are added.   Remove from fire and beat all
together well.   Set aside until mixture is cool, then
shape into balls and flatten to cylinders.   Roll in
crumbs, white of egg diluted with water, crumbs
again.   Fry from a basket in deep fat at 390° F.
The croquettes should be soft and luscious inside
with a golden brown covering.

CHEESE AND POTATO CROQUETTES

2 cups mashed white potato	1 egg yolk, beaten
2 tablespoons grated cheese	1 tablespoon milk
Salt, onion juice	

Mix in order given and season to taste.   Mold into
balls or cylinders.   Cover with crumbs; dip in
beaten egg white, diluted with water, then in crumbs
again, and fry in deep fat, at 390° F.

CHEESE DREAMS

Dice a half pound of soft cheese.   Mix to a paste
with a tablespoon of butter and a teaspoon of made
mustard.   Cover neatly trimmed slices of stale bread
with the cheese paste.   Make a batter as for
French toast of one egg slightly beaten, a pinch of
salt, and a half cup of milk.   Cover each cheese-
slice of bread with a plain slice and dip into the milk

mixture. Melt a tablespoon of butter in a saucepan and sauté the sandwiches on both sides until nicely browned and soft. They may be cut into strips for serving or used whole. If fresh bread is used, sandwiches may be made with the cheese paste and set into a hot oven until toasted and the cheese creamy.

"CHARLEY'S" WELSH RAREBIT

1 pound snappy cheese	½ cup milk
⅛ teaspoon mustard	1 egg slightly beaten
¼ teaspoon cayenne	Crusader crackers
¼ teaspoon Worcestershire Sauce	

Melt the cheese in a double boiler. Add the seasonings and cook together over hot water. Put in the milk and beaten egg. Stir and cook together for about three minutes. Serve on Crusader crackers or prepared toast.

TOMATO CHEESE RAREBIT

1 cup stewed or fresh chopped tomatoes	2 tablespoons butter
⅓ teaspoon soda	2 tablespoons flour
½ teaspoon mustard	¾ cup milk
	2 cups cheese cut fine
1 egg	

Cook the tomatoes with the seasonings and strain. In a separate dish melt the butter and cheese. Stir in the flour and milk gradually and cook until smooth. Add the soda and beaten egg to the tomato. Combine mixtures. Heat together thoroughly and serve on toast or crackers.

CHEESE SOUFFLÉ

2 eggs separated	2 cups milk
1 cup bread crumbs	1 cup grated cheese

Butter, salt

Soak the bread crumbs in the milk three minutes. Beat the egg yolks and stir in. Add the cheese and last of all the stiffly beaten egg whites folded in. Pour into a buttered baking dish of just the right size — one which may be sent to table. Cover the top with fine bread crumbs and plenty of butter in small bits. Bake about half an hour or until a nice brown, in a hot oven, or at 400° F.

CHEESE STRAWS

Roll remnants of pie paste until thin. Cover thickly with grated cheese and season with paprika. Fold over. Sprinkle on more cheese and paprika. Fold and roll to a quarter inch in thickness. Cut into long, narrow strips, about a third inch in width and five inches long. Place in a baking pan, pressing down each end of the strips to prevent their shrinking. Serve, piled log-cabin style, with the salad course.

COTTAGE CHEESE

Set three or more quarts of sour milk in a warm place or over hot water until the curd separates from the whey. Place a square of cheesecloth over a strainer and drain. Gather up the corners of the cloth and hang for several hours. Turn the cheese into a bowl; beat in a little cream or a piece of butter, a little salt, and mold into cakes.

CAKES AND COOKIES

ANGEL CAKE — "AMRITA"

6 egg whites	1 teaspoon cream of tartar
¾ cup pastry flour	1 scant cup sifted sugar
½ teaspoon vanilla	

Beat the whites to a stiff froth with a pinch of salt. Sift flour and cream of tartar five times. Add the sugar to the egg whites very gradually and mix in the flour and vanilla flavoring. Dust lightly with flour a small angel-cake tin — one with a tube in the middle — and pour in the mixture. Bake in a slow oven — at 325° F. — about half an hour. When well risen, an oiled paper over the top will prevent too quick browning.

ANGEL SPONGE CAKE

4 eggs, separated	1 dessertspoon vinegar
1 cup sugar	1 cup flour
1 tablespoon water	1 extra tablespoon water

Beat whites of the eggs with a tablespoon of water until stiff. Add sugar and beat again. Mix the yolks with one tablespoon water and one of vinegar and beat until lemon-colored. Bake forty minutes with gradually increasing heat.   Inspect at end of first twenty minutes.

APPLE SAUCE CAKE

½ cup apple sauce	2 cups flour
1 cup sugar	1 cup seeded raisins
½ cup sour cream	1 teaspoon each, nutmeg,
1 teaspoon soda	cinnamon, and cloves

Mix together apple sauce, sugar, and cream.   Stir in the soda until dissolved.   Cut up the raisins and lightly flour them.   Sift in the flour and spices. Add raisins last.   Bake in a slow oven — 325° F.   A half cup of nut meats may be added with the raisins, if desired.

BABY CREAM PUFFS

1 cup boiling water	1¼ cups flour
2 tablespoons butter	4 eggs
1 tablespoon sugar	

Put into a saucepan over the fire the water, butter, and sugar.   When dissolved, add the flour all at once, and stir vigorously.   Remove from fire, and when somewhat cooled, add the unbeaten eggs, one at a time, and beat hard as each is added.   The mixture is right when it will hold its shape and not spread too quickly when dropped from a spoon. Use a pastry bag with plain tube for shaping the puffs.   Make little mounds not over an inch in diameter, using a buttered baking pan of large size.

If a glaze is liked, brush over the tops with beaten egg. Bake in a hot oven, starting at 450° F. until puffed and brown, then reduce to 325° F. and finish baking. The cakes must be thoroughly cooked before removing, as otherwise they will fall. When cool, make a slit in the side and fill with cream filling, or whipped or mocha cream. Ice-cream filling with a hot chocolate sauce makes a delectable dessert.

BRIDGE PARTY BROWNIES

2 squares Baker's chocolate	2 eggs
2 tablespoons butter	2 tablespoons flour
1 cup sugar	1 cup chopped walnuts
1 teaspoon vanilla	

Melt chocolate over hot water. Add butter and sugar. Remove from heat. Beat in the eggs. Sift in the flour. Add nuts and flavoring. Bake in a shallow pan and cut into squares while still warm.

DUMP CAKE

2 eggs	1½ cups flour
Butter size of an egg	1 cup sugar
2 teaspoons baking powder	Milk, flavoring

This very good and quickly made cake has reappeared of late years as "Hurry-Up Cake." Melt the butter in a measuring cup. Break in the two eggs unbeaten. Fill the cup with sweet milk. Sift baking powder with flour. Mix with sugar and into this "dump" the egg mixture. Beat all together for five full minutes. Bake in a small, rather deep, greased pan, in a moderate oven, or at 350° F.

EGGLESS CAKE

1 cup brown sugar	2 cups bread flour
½ cup lard or Crisco	1 teaspoon soda
2 cups seeded raisins	1 teaspoon baking powder
1 cup hot water	½ cup nut meats
½ teaspoon salt	1 teaspoon vanilla

This cake is not only without eggs, but also without butter or milk. It keeps moist a long time, and is very good.

Place the sugar, lard, raisins, and water over the fire. Add half a teaspoon each of cloves, nutmeg, and mace, with two teaspoons cinnamon.

Cook slowly five minutes. Let cool and add remaining ingredients. Beat two full minutes. Bake in a moderate oven in fruit cake tin, about fifty minutes.

WIANNO FUDGE CAKE

5 squares unsweetened chocolate	½ cup milk
5 tablespoons boiling water	1¾ cups flour sifted
½ cup butter	1 teaspoon baking powder
1½ cups sugar	4 eggs separated
	1 teaspoon vanilla

Dissolve chocolate in boiling water. Beat butter to a cream. Add sugar and beaten egg yolks. Mix in the milk thoroughly. Add the dissolved chocolate and water, and the flour gradually. Beat egg whites stiff and stir in gently. Flavor with vanilla.

Bake in two layer-cake tins or in one loaf as preferred. This is also a good recipe for small cakes. Ice and fill with Fudge Cake Frosting. (See Cake Fillings.)

LYDIA'S GINGERBREAD

1 cup molasses	1 egg
Butter size of an egg	2¼ cups flour (pastry)
½ cup sour cream	2 teaspoons ginger
1 level teaspoon soda	A little mace
Salt	

Mix molasses and butter melted. Add beaten egg. Dissolve soda in cream. Add to molasses. Sift in flour with spices and salt last. Bake in a moderate oven or at 350° F.

OLD-FASHIONED HERMITS

½ cup butter or substitute	1 teaspoon soda
1½ cups brown sugar	1 cup raisins
2 tablespoons sour milk	1 cup currants
2 eggs	½ teaspoon each nutmeg
3 cups pastry flour	and cinnamon

Cream butter and add sugar gradually. Beat eggs and add with milk. Sift soda and half the flour together and mix in. Chop and flour the raisins and currants. Sift the spices with remainder of flour. Combine all and beat well. Drop by spoonfuls on a greased tin, leaving a little space between for spreading. Bake about fifteen minutes, in a moderate oven, or at 350° F.

IRA'S CHOCOLATE CAKE

¼ cup butter	1¼ cups sifted flour
1 cup sugar	½ cup sour milk
2 eggs	2 squares chocolate
1 teaspoon soda	¼ cup hot water

Vanilla flavoring

Beat together butter, sugar, and eggs. Sift soda into flour. Combine and add sour milk, chocolate, and vanilla. Last of all the water, very gradually. Ice with white or chocolate icing.

CHOCOLATE CUP CAKES

1 cup brown sugar	1 cup flour
¼ cup shortening	½ teaspoon baking powder
1 egg well beaten	¼ cup cocoa
¼ cup sour milk	¼ cup water
½ teaspoon soda	Vanilla

Cream the sugar and shortening. If butter is not used, add salt. Dissolve soda in the milk and the cocoa in cold water, until smooth. Sift baking powder with flour and combine ingredients. This makes twelve cakes in muffin tins — which should be well buttered. Bake in a moderate oven or at 350° F. Ice with chocolate or white icing.

BANBURY TARTS

1 cup chopped raisins	1 lemon, juice and grated rind
1 large apple, peeled and chopped fine	¾ cup sugar
	1 egg

Cook ingredients together slowly for twelve minutes. Let cool. Roll out thin squares of pastry. Place a tablespoon of filling on half of one side and fold over, pressing edges well together. Make a few gashes on top. Bake in quick oven, 400° F.

SOFT CREAM COOKIES

¼ cup butter	1 teaspoon soda
1½ cups sugar	2½ cups bread flour
2 eggs beaten light	2 teaspoons grated nutmeg
1 cup sour cream	Salt

Cream together butter, sugar, and eggs. Beat hard. Mix sour cream with soda and add. Sift in bread flour and salt. Add nutmeg or other flavoring. If liked soft, do not use more flour in rolling out. Place them some distance apart in baking tin as they spread in cooking. Sprinkle with sugar and water when placing in the oven if a little crust is liked. This recipe makes twenty-five to twenty-eight cookies. Bake in a moderate oven — 350° F.

THIN SUGAR COOKIES

⅓ cup butter	2 cups flour
⅔ cup sugar	2 teaspoons baking powder
2 tablespoons milk	½ teaspoon salt

Cream butter and sugar. Sift baking powder and salt into flour. Combine. Roll very thin. Sprinkle with sugar before cutting out. Bake at 350° F.

HYANNIS SUGAR COOKIES

⅔ cup shortening	2 cups flour
1⅓ cups sugar	2 teaspoons baking powder
2 tablespoons milk	¼ teaspoon salt
2 eggs	¼ teaspoon nutmeg

1 teaspoon lemon extract

Cream the butter or other shortening. Add sugar, beaten eggs, milk, and lemon flavoring. Beat two minutes. Sift together flour, baking powder, and salt. Add the nutmeg and combine mixtures. Turn out on a floured board. Roll quarter of an inch thick. Cut out and place half an inch apart on a greased sheet. Bake about ten minutes in moderate oven. In order to avoid stiffening the cookies, it is well to reserve a portion of the flour to be taken up in rolling out.

NANNIE'S MOLASSES COOKIES

2 cups molasses	1 tablespoon water
1 cup sugar	1 teaspoon ginger
1 cup shortening	A little cinnamon and salt
1 teaspoon soda	Flour to roll out

Bring to a boil the molasses, sugar, and shortening which may be half butter and half lard. Remove from fire and add the soda dissolved in water, the spices, and the flour. This will require two or more cups of bread flour. Roll thin. Cut out and bake in quick oven or at 350° F.

THE CAP'N'S FILLED COOKIES

½ cup butter or substitute
1 cup sugar
1 egg
½ cup milk

1 teaspoon soda
2 teaspoons cream of tartar
3½ cups flour in all
Vanilla

Mix and roll into very thin sheet. Cut into rounds. Place a spoonful of filling on one round and cover with another. Wet and pinch the edges together. Bake in quick oven, or at 350° F.

Filling

1 cup chopped raisins
½ cup sugar

½ cup water
1 teaspoon flour

Cook until thick. Cool a little before using.

DOUGHNUTS

1 cup sugar
2 teaspoons melted shortening
2 eggs beaten
1 cup milk

½ teaspoon salt
4 teaspoons baking powder
3½ cups flour
Nutmeg, vanilla

Mix sugar and shortening. Beat eggs and add. Sift baking powder with flour and add alternately with milk. Add spices and remainder of flour. Roll on floured board. Cut with doughnut cutter and drop into deep fat heated to 375° F. This should be in an iron kettle. Take out doughnuts with a fork and place on paper to drain. Sprinkle with sugar if so liked.

RAISED DOUGHNUTS — "SPRING HILL"

1¼ cups milk scalded and cooled	1 yeast cake
1 teaspoon salt	1½ cups flour
1 cup sugar	1 egg
2 tablespoons melted butter	Nutmeg, cinnamon
	2 extra cups flour

Mix the scalded milk, a teaspoon of salt and the melted butter. Let cool. Dissolve the yeast cake in a little water. Stir in with one and a half cups flour. Beat well and let rise about an hour. Then beat in the egg and spices, and remainder of flour. Let rise again. Roll on floured board to half an inch in thickness. Cut out and let rise once more. Then fry in deep fat, as for plain doughnuts.

NUT LAYER CAKE

1 cup sugar	2 eggs, well beaten
½ cup butter	1 teaspoon cream of tartar
½ cup milk	½ teaspoon soda
2 cups flour	1 cup chopped raisins
1 cup chopped walnuts	

Cream the butter and sugar. Add a pinch of salt. Dissolve the soda in the milk and add with the beaten eggs. Sift cream of tartar with the flour and stir in gradually. Add spices and the floured raisins and chopped nut meats. Bake in two layer-cake tins in a moderate oven. Use "Nut Cake Filling" to spread between the layers and on top.

OATMEAL WAFERS

2 cups rolled oats	2 eggs
1 cup flour	4 tablespoons milk
1 teaspoon soda	1 cup chopped nut meats
¼ cup butter	¼ teaspoon each salt, cinnamon,
1 cup light brown sugar	cloves, and nutmeg

Sift together the dry ingredients except sugar. Cream butter, add sugar, beaten eggs, milk, flour, and rolled oats. Beat well. Put in the nut meats and beat again. Drop from tip of a teaspoon on a buttered sheet about two inches apart. Bake in quick oven at 350° F. for ten minutes, taking care not to burn.

WALNUT WAFERS

1 cup brown sugar	¼ teaspoon baking powder
2 rounded tablespoons flour	2 eggs unbeaten
1 cup broken walnut meats	

Mix and drop from a spoon on a buttered sheet. Bake in a slow oven — 325° F. ten minutes. A tablespoon of melted chocolate may be added to vary the flavor.

SPICE CAKE — "SEWING CIRCLE"

2 cups sifted flour	1 teaspoon cinnamon
1 egg well beaten	¾ cup milk
1¼ cups brown sugar	½ teaspoon allspice
¼ cup butter	¼ each cloves, nutmeg,
4 teaspoons baking powder	salt and ginger
1 cup raisins, seeded	

Cream butter and sugar. Add the beaten egg. Sift flour and baking powder, salt, and spices three times. Add to the butter and egg alternating with the milk. Beat thoroughly to a smooth mixture. Flour the raisins and stir in. Bake in a buttered loaf-cake tin about one hour. Moderate oven. Frost with Divinity or boiled frosting.

SOUR MILK SPICE CAKE

1 cup sugar	1 teaspoon soda
1 cup butter or substitute	1 cup raisins
1 cup sour milk	1 teaspoon each of all
2 eggs	kinds of spices
1 cup molasses	Flour to mix

Mix in the usual manner, adding flour to make a good cake batter, not too stiff. Beat well before baking. This is good with a boiled white frosting on top and sides.

PARTY SPONGE CAKES

4 eggs, yolks separated	2 tablespoons cornstarch
3 tablespoons cold water	1 scant cup pastry flour
1 cup sugar	1¼ teaspoons baking powder
1 teaspoon lemon extract	⅛ teaspoon salt

Beat yolks until lemon colored, adding the cold water. Add sugar and extract. Beat again. Mix together flour, cornstarch, salt, and baking powder. Sift well. Fold into yolks. Whip the whites stiff and cut them in. Grease small muffin tins and dust with flour. Fill two thirds full. Bake about twenty minutes in moderate oven at 350° F. Let cakes stand a few minutes before removing from the tins.

SURPRISE CAKES

Line gem tins with pastry. Drop a spoonful of any kind of jelly into each one. Cover with a heaping spoonful of a plain cake batter. Bake as a cake at 375° F.

OLD-FASHIONED STRAWBERRY SHORTCAKE

2 cups sifted flour	1 teaspoon sugar
½ teaspoon salt	4 tablespoons butter
4 teaspoons baking powder	¾ cup milk or part water

Sift together the dry ingredients. Work the butter into the flour with tips of the fingers. Add the liquid gradually, using a knife for mixing instead of a spoon. Divide dough into halves and roll each half out lightly on a floured board to a half inch or so in thickness. Shape to a round, buttered tin. Spread one layer in the tin. Brush over with melted butter. Put on the other layer. Bake in quick oven or at 450° F. about twelve minutes. Pull apart when done. Spread generously with melted butter and crushed berries sweetened with sugar. Place more berries on top. Serve with Berry Butter or whipped cream. For individual shortcakes, cut the dough with a large biscuit cutter. Bake and split while hot. Spread between and on top with crushed berries. Shortcakes may be made with blueberries, raspberries, or peaches in the same fashion.

CAKE FILLINGS AND FROSTINGS

ANGEL CAKE ICING

¼ cup granulated sugar   Confectioners' sugar
½ cup boiling water

Boil granulated sugar and water together three minutes. Remove from fire and stir in confectioners' sugar until of right consistency to spread. This icing will not run off.

CHOCOLATE ICING

Melt two squares of chocolate in a saucepan over hot water. Remove from heat and stir in confectioners' sugar until stiff. Thin with two tablespoons warm milk. Add two more tablespoons of sugar and two more tablespoons of milk, until icing is soft enough to spread easily.

FUDGE CAKE FROSTING

2 squares chocolate   1 teaspoon butter
½ cup milk   2 cups confectioners' sugar
1 egg yolk   1 teaspoonful vanilla

Put all the ingredients into a pan over boiling water. Beat until smooth and glossy. Remove from fire and continue beating until ready to use.

When used as a filling, chopped nuts may be added as a variation.

FUDGE FROSTING

4 squares chocolate   ⅓ cup warm milk
2½ cups confectioners' sugar   Vanilla

Melt chocolate over hot water. Stir in sugar until stiff. Thin with a few teaspoons of the milk. Beat hard. Add more sugar, then more milk until all is used. If it becomes too thick at last, set pan over hot water until it melts again. Hard beating is necessary for a smooth frosting.

CREAM FILLING

2 eggs   1 scant cup sugar
2 cups milk, scalded   ⅓ cup flour
Salt, vanilla

Mix sugar and flour. Beat eggs slightly. Scald milk and combine. Cook in double boiler about fifteen minutes, stirring until it thickens. When nearly cool, add flavoring.

MARSHMALLOW FILLING

Cut marshmallows into thirds crosswise. Cover the cake while it is still warm. Pour Fudge Frosting over the marshmallows.

MOCHA ICING AND FILLING

3 tablespoons hot black coffee   3 tablespoons cocoa
1½ tablespoons butter   1 teaspoon vanilla
                Confectioners' sugar

Mix coffee, butter, and cocoa.   Boil three minutes.
Cool.   Add vanilla and enough confectioners' sugar
to spread easily over required layers.

NUT CAKE FILLING

Mix two tablespoons marshmallow cream with
one cup of chopped raisins and confectioners' sugar
to sweeten.   Use lemon juice to make of right consistency to spread.

BOILED FROSTING

2 cups white sugar   2 egg whites, beaten stiff
1 cup water   ⅛ teaspoon cream of tartar
                1 teaspoon vanilla extract

Boil sugar, water, and cream of tartar together
over a slow fire until the syrup will spin a thread
when dropped from a spoon.   Do not stir while
boiling.   Pour slowly upon the stiffly beaten egg
whites.   Beat until frosting cools, when it should be
thick and fluffy.   Add vanilla last.

DIVINITY FROSTING

3 cups sugar   1 teaspoon white corn syrup
1⅓ cups boiling water   4 egg whites, stiffly beaten
                1 teaspoon vanilla flavoring

Place over a slow fire the sugar, water, and corn syrup. Stir constantly until dissolved. Boil until the syrup spins a long thread or makes a soft ball in cold water. Pour slowly over the egg whites and beat constantly. When it cools, add the vanilla and beat again. Spread on chocolate cake or between layers.

PIES

APPLE PIE

2½ or 3 cups tart apples	Rind and juice of ½ lemon
¾ cup sugar	⅛ teaspoon salt
¼ teaspoon cinnamon	1 teaspoon butter

Line a pie plate with a thin crust. Peel and quarter apples to fill the plate, slicing each quarter twice again. Arrange them evenly on the plate, beginning at the edge and working toward the middle, where they should be thicker. Sprinkle on the sugar and seasonings. Dot with bits of butter. Wet edges of lower crust before putting on the perforated upper crust. Bake until nicely browned, in a hot oven, or at 450° F. until the crust is brown, then moderate to 350° F. and finish baking.

DEEP DISH APPLE PIE

5 or 6 tart apples	⅓ teaspoon grated nutmeg
¾ to 1 cup sugar	Salt

Cut apples into eighths after peeling. Arrange as for apple pie in a deep baking dish but without under crust. Sprinkle over them sugar, nutmeg, and bits of butter. Cover with a rich perforated upper crust. Bake about forty-five minutes. Serve hot with plain cream.

BANANA CUSTARD PIE

1 cup bananas	1 cup milk
½ cup sugar	1 egg
Juice 1 lemon	1 egg yolk
½ teaspoon grated rind	Nutmeg

Rub the bananas through a sieve.   Add the sugar to the pulp with lemon juice and rind.   Beat the eggs slightly and stir in with the milk and nutmeg. Line a deep pie plate with pastry and pour in the mixture.   Bake twenty-five minutes in slow oven. To be eaten cold.

BLUEBERRY PIE

1 quart blueberries	1 tablespoon flour
⅛ teaspoon salt	1 tablespoon butter
1 cup sugar	

Wash and select the berries.   Drain well.   Mix them with salt, sugar, and flour.   Prepare a deep pie plate with a pastry under crust.   Turn in the berries. Dot over with bits of butter.   Put on a rich perforated upper crust.   Bake until flaky and light brown.   Use oven temperatures as in Apple Pie.

CHERRY PIE NUMBER I

2½ cups cherries, stoned	2½ tablespoons flour
1 cup sugar	Pastry

Mix sugar and flour together and add to cherries. Line a deep plate with pastry and pour in the cherries. Dot with bits of butter. Place perforated upper crust and bake like Apple Pie.

CHERRY PIE NUMBER II

5 cups stoned cherries	1½ tablespoons flour
⅓ cup water	2 tablespoons butter
2 cups sugar	⅛ teaspoon salt
¼ teaspoon cinnamon	

This pie requires a very deep dish. Cook cherries and water together five minutes. Mix sugar, flour, and salt, and add. Bring to a boil and continue for three minutes. Set aside to cool. Line the pie dish with paste. Pour in the filling. Dot over with the bits of butter. Sprinkle with powdered cinnamon. Wet edges of under crust and place the perforated upper crust, pinching the edges together well to prevent escaping juice. Bake in moderately hot oven about half an hour, or until the crust shrinks from sides of the plate.

COCONUT CUSTARD PIE

2 eggs slightly beaten	1 cup dessicated coconut
4 tablespoons sugar	⅛ teaspoon salt
2 cups milk	Nutmeg

Mix together sugar and eggs. Stir in the milk, coconut, salt, and nutmeg. When well mixed, pour into a pie plate lined with good pastry. Bake about forty-five minutes in moderate oven, or at 350° F.

CRANBERRY PIE

1½ cups cranberries   2 tablespoons sifted bread
⅔ cup water   crumbs or flour
1 cup sugar   ¼ teaspoon salt

Cook the berries, sugar, and water together for
ten minutes, stirring often to break up the berries.
Add the salt, crumbs, or flour. Cook a moment,
then remove and cool.   Line a pie plate with pastry.
Pour in the berries.   Cover the top with latticed
strips of the paste and bake until nicely browned.

WINTER FRUIT PIE

2 cups chopped apples   ½ cup water
2 cups dried currants   1 teaspoon butter
1 large cup sugar   1 teaspoon vanilla

Mix in order given.   Make a rich crust for top and
bottom.   Dust over the filling with flour before
putting on the top crust.   Bake like Apple Pie.

LEMON CUSTARD OR CAKE PIE

1 lemon, juice and grated   1 heaping tablespoon flour
   rind   1 teaspoon melted butter
1 cup sugar   1 cup milk
Yolks 2 eggs   Whites of 2 eggs, beaten stiff

Mix in order given, folding in the egg whites carefully.   Bake in one crust in rather slow oven as the
cakelike mixture must be allowed to rise before
browning.   A delicious pie.

LEMON MERINGUE PIE — "OPECHEE"

4 tablespoons flour
3 tablespoons cornstarch
1 cup sugar
⅛ teaspoon salt
3 eggs, yolks separated

2 lemons, juice and grated rind
1 tablespoon butter
3 heaping tablespoons powdered sugar

1¼ cups boiling water

Mix flour, salt, cornstarch, and sugar. Put them in a saucepan on the fire. Stir in the boiling water very gradually. When boiling and well mixed, set pan over hot water. Beat the egg yolks and stir in. Cook until set but do not allow to boil. Take from the fire and beat in the lemon juice and rind and melted butter. Have ready a baked under crust (may be baked over an inverted pie plate to hold shape). Pour in the mixture.

Make a meringue of the stiffly beaten egg whites and powdered sugar. Place on top. Bake fifteen or twenty minutes in slow oven until a delicate brown.

MINCE PIE

See "Mince Meat" for filling. Make a rich crust for top and bottom. Fill with the mince meat. Place bits of butter over the filling and put on a perforated top. Brush over with milk to give a brown crust. Bake like Apple Pie.

PUMPKIN PIE — "CHATHAM BARS"

1½ cups steamed, strained pumpkin
⅔ cup brown sugar
½ teaspoon ginger
½ teaspoon cinnamon or nutmeg

2 eggs
1½ cups milk
½ teaspoon salt
½ cup cream

Mix in order given. Bake in one crust about forty minutes. The oven should be fairly hot at first — 500° F. — then heat reduced to 350° F. for remainder of baking.

RHUBARB PIE — "BREWSTER"

4 cups rhubarb, diced
1 cup sugar

1 tablespoon lemon juice
1 tablespoon butter

1 egg

Mix as given and bake with under crust only, rolled thin and fitted to a deep pie plate. Use the butter to dot over the filling before putting on the top pieces of lattice strips cut from the pastry. Bake like Apple Pie.

RHUBARB PIE — "QUISSET"

2 cups rhubarb
1 cup sugar

¼ cup sifted bread crumbs
2 tablespoons sultana raisins

Salt, nutmeg

Dice the rhubarb. Scald it with boiling water while in a strainer. Line a pie plate with good paste. Put in the ingredients with bits of butter on top. Cover with a perforated upper crust and bake.

RAISIN PIE

1 cup seeded raisins	1 cup water
1 cup sugar	2 lemons, juice and grated
1 heaping tablespoon flour	rind
1½ cups molasses	⅛ teaspoon salt

Mix the flour and sugar. Add the molasses, water, lemon juice, and rind. Season. Stir in the raisins slightly floured. Bake between two crusts like Apple Pie.

SWEET POTATO PIE

4 large baked sweet potatoes	3 eggs beaten
2 tablespoons butter	1 cup milk
2 tablespoons sugar	Nutmeg, salt

Mash the potatoes. Beat until light. Add the butter and sugar. Beat again. Stir in the well-beaten eggs. Warm the milk and add with seasonings. Bake like a pumpkin pie in lower crust only.

PUDDINGS

APPLE SNOW PUDDING

1 cup apple pulp	1 tablespoon lemon juice
3 egg whites	½ cup sugar

Pare and quarter the apples. Steam them until soft enough to be rubbed through a sieve. Beat egg whites until stiff. Fold in the sugar and apple pulp mixed with lemon juice. Serve with cold Custard Sauce in glass dishes.

BAKED APPLES

Select six or eight firm and rather tart apples. Polish them. Cut off the stem ends and remove cores. Fill the cavities with sugar mixed with cinnamon. Place bits of butter on top. Put them into a pan with half a cup of water and half a cup of sugar. Bake in a moderate oven — 375° F. Baste occasionally with the syrup in the pan. The apples may be pared, if preferred, and cooked in the same fashion. There are many possible fillings:

Fill cavities with seeded raisins and chopped nuts, and sweeten with brown sugar.

Use red cinnamon candies in place of sugar.

Fill with sugar. Add chopped marshmallows when the apples begin to grow tender. These will melt and make a creamy sauce.

Blushing apples are very pretty, made by filling unpeeled apples with cranberry jelly, and basting with the cranberry syrup while baking.

APPLE SLUMP — OLD RECIPE

Butter a deep earthenware pudding dish. Fill it nearly full with pared and quartered apples. Sprinkle with half a cup of sugar and a little powdered cinnamon. Make a rich biscuit dough and cover pie with it. Bake in a hot oven — 400° F. — until brown. Then invert on a hot plate. The apples will be on top. Dot them over with bits of butter and more sugar and cinnamon. Serve hot with Hard Sauce.

BAKED APPLE DUMPLINGS — "BELMONT"

Make a rich pie crust. Core and pare apples, one for each person. Replace the core of each apple with one tablespoon sugar and a bit of butter. Cut pastry into squares large enough to wrap up the apple. Wet the edges of the squares and pinch them together to prevent separating in baking. Place the dumplings in a buttered pan, adding cold water to half cover them. Add also, for each apple, one tablespoon sugar, and one quarter of a teaspoon grated nutmeg. Cover the pan closely and bake in a moderate oven — 350° F. — for two hours. Remove cover at end of first hour. The syrup in the pan will be found delicious.

OLD-FASHIONED BIRD'S NEST PUDDING

Pare and core five or six nice apples. Butter a pudding dish and place the apples in it. Mix five teaspoons of flour with one teaspoon salt, and wet to a paste with cold milk, from the pint to be used altogether. Beat yolks of three eggs and stir in. Fold in the stiffly beaten egg whites. Add remainder of the milk and pour all over the apples. Bake in slow oven — 325° F. — about one hour. Serve with a hot sweet sauce.

CINNAMON APPLES — "WESTLOOK"

6 rather tart apples of uniform size
1 cup sugar
1 cup water
2 heaping tablespoons red cinnamon candies

This is a very pretty and easily prepared dessert. Make a syrup of the sugar and water. Put in the red candies and stir until melted. Pare and core the apples. Cook them whole in the red syrup, turning and basting them until tender. Use a graniteware or enamel dish on top of the stove. When cooked, the apples will be covered with a red glaze. Cool before using. Serve in sherbet glasses with unsweetened cream.

APRICOT WHIP

1 cup cooked apricots	1 tablespoon lemon juice
¼ cup apricot juice	3 egg whites
½ cup sugar	⅛ teaspoon salt

Cook apricots, sugar, and juice together until like thick marmalade. Cool. Stir in the lemon juice. Beat egg whites stiff with the salt. Add apricot mixture and beat all until creamy. Pile in sherbet cups and set aside to chill. Serve with whipped cream or cold Custard Sauce.

BERRY GRUNT — "OLD NANTUCKET"

Cook a pint or more of berries in a minimum amount of water until soft but not broken. Make a dough of one and a half cups flour, one teaspoon butter, two heaping teaspoons baking powder, with milk to mix.

Fill a deep yellow baking dish with the berries slightly sweetened. Place the dough on top of berries and set dish into a kettle of boiling water, coming to within an inch of the top. Cook steadily about an hour. On no account must the water stop boiling, as this would cause the dough to fall. This is a very old Nantucket recipe, varied according to the berries in season.   Blueberries and huckleberries were the most used.   Nutmeg Sauce often served. See Pudding Sauces.

BAKED INDIAN PUDDING

⅓ cup Indian or corn meal	½ cup molasses
5 cups scalded milk	1 teaspoon salt

1 teaspoon ginger

Pour milk slowly over the meal.   Cook in double boiler twenty minutes.   Add remaining ingredients. Pour into buttered baking dish.   Set in a pan of hot water.   Bake two hours in slow oven.   Delicious with plain or whipped cream, and good, hot or cold.

BAKED PEARS

After washing the pears, set them close together in a buttered baking dish, stems up.   Mix half a teaspoon powdered ginger with half a cup of sugar and sprinkle over them.   Pour half a cup of water into the pan.   Bake until tender and brown.   Serve cold with syrup from the pan.

BROWN BETTY

Butter a baking dish.   Line it with apples sliced thin after peeling.   Cover with a thick layer of bread crumbs sprinkled with brown sugar, bits of butter, and cinnamon.   Repeat until dish is nearly full. Cover all with thick sweet apple sauce. Bake forty minutes in moderate oven, or at 350° F.

IRISH MOSS BLANCMANGE

½ cup Irish moss   1 quart milk
¼ teaspoon salt

Wash the moss in several waters to remove sand. Place it with the milk in double boiler and cook half an hour. Add salt and flavor with vanilla or lemon. Strain into molds and set aside to become firm. It should not be stirred after straining. The moss may be tied in a coarse netting while cooking. If milk is not plentiful, cook the moss in a pint of water. Strain and mix with a pint of scalded milk. The moss may be purchased at drug stores if one is not near the seashore, where it is often left by the receding tide.

BUTTERSCOTCH TAPIOCA

¼ cup tapioca   3 tablespoons butter
⅛ teaspoon salt   6 tablespoons brown sugar
2 cups milk, scalded   1 egg white beaten stiff
1 egg yolk, beaten

Cook milk, salt, and tapioca fifteen minutes in a double boiler. Beat egg yolk and pour over a small amount of the mixture. Return all to double boiler and cook until it thickens. In a small sauce pan melt butter, add sugar, and stir carefully until melted.

Add to mixture in double boiler. Stir to blend, then remove from stove and fold in beaten egg white. Set aside to chill. Serve in sherbet glasses with whipped cream on top. A little minced preserved ginger gives a different flavor, or chopped nuts may be used.

CARAMEL BREAD PUDDING

¾ cup brown sugar	¼ teaspoon salt
2 tablespoons butter	1½ cups bread bits
2 cups milk	¼ cup brown sugar
2 eggs, yolks separated	Vanilla flavoring

Caramelize the sugar slightly by cooking with butter alone for two minutes. Put into double boiler over hot water. Add the milk and scald. Beat egg yolks with salt and stir in slowly. Butter a deep pudding dish, put in the buttered bread bits and pour the hot mixture over them. Set into moderate oven — 350° F. — to bake until firm. Make a meringue of the beaten egg whites folded into the brown sugar — quarter of a cup. Flavor and place on top of pudding. Set into oven to brown about eight minutes.

CHOCOLATE SOUFFLÉ — "BUZZARD'S BAY"

2 tablespoons melted butter	⅓ cup sugar
2 tablespoons flour	3 eggs, yolks separated
¾ cup scalded milk	2 tablespoons hot water
2 squares Baker's chocolate	Vanilla flavoring

Blend melted butter and flour, using top part of double boiler. Pour milk on gradually. Stir and cook until thick. In a small saucepan over hot water melt the chocolate. Add sugar and water and stir until smooth. Then combine mixtures. Beat yolks of the eggs until light and stir in. Let cool and fold in the whites of the eggs beaten stiff. Add a half teaspoon of vanilla. Bake in buttered baking dish which may be sent to table, for twenty-five minutes in a moderate oven. Be sure the top center of the soufflé is firm before taking from oven. Soufflés must be served immediately or they will fall. Serve with Hard Sauce or whipped cream.

NANTUCKET CRACKER PUDDING — "MOUNTAIN DEW"

4 common crackers	1 tablespoon butter
1 quart milk	¾ cup sugar
3 eggs, yolks separated	Salt, vanilla

Use a rolling pin to pulverize the crackers. Mix them with sugar, salt, and milk. Beat egg yolks and stir in. Add the butter. Bake in a deep baking dish about an hour. Make a meringue of two egg whites beaten stiff and two tablespoons powdered sugar. Place on top of pudding and set into oven to brown.

BAKED DATE PUDDING

1 cup sugar	½ cup milk
2 eggs, beaten	½ cup nut meats
1 cup bread crumbs	¾ cup dates
1 teaspoon baking powder	½ teaspoon salt

Mix together sugar and eggs, well beaten. Cut the dates and nut meats into bits. Combine ingredients in a well-buttered pudding dish. Bake half an hour in a slow oven or at 300° F. Serve with plain or whipped cream.

BAKED PRUNE PUDDING

Make like Baked Date Pudding, substituting pitted prunes for the dates.

FLOATING ISLAND PUDDING

4 eggs, slightly beaten	1 quart milk, scalded
½ cup sugar	Vanilla flavoring
¼ teaspoon salt	

Make a custard by mixing eggs, sugar, and salt. Pour on the hot milk gradually. Cook and stir in double boiler until it will coat a spoon. Strain. Flavor. Set away to cool. When about to serve, make small individual meringues for the top as follows: two egg whites, beaten stiff, four tablespoons sugar, one tablespoon lemon juice. Mix and drop from tip of a spoon upon the soft custard.

HUCKLEBERRY SLUMP

Wash and prepare a quart or more of berries. Add sugar to sweeten. Heat until softened. Into this hot sauce drop dumplings made of biscuit dough. Cook until the dumplings are done. They will puff up in the sauce. Serve with berries poured over the dumplings and plain cream.

ICE-BOX PUDDING — "AMRITA"

4 ounces "Dot" chocolate	4 eggs, yolks separated
7 tablespoons powdered sugar	1 teaspoon vanilla
2 tablespoons hot water	½ pound lady fingers

Melt the chocolate in a double boiler; add sugar and water. Stir until smooth. Remove from fire and beat in the egg yolks one at a time. Beat the whites stiff and fold in with the vanilla. Line a loaf bread pan with waxed paper; arrange a layer of lady fingers, then a layer of the mixture until all is used. Set into ice box for use on following day. When served, cover top with un-sweetened whipped cream.

NUT AND FIG PUDDING, STEAMED

⅓ cup butter	⅛ pound figs, chopped
½ cup molasses	½ cup walnut meats
½ cup milk	1½ teaspoons soda
1¾ cups bread flour	¼ teaspoon each, cloves, cinna-
1¼ cups seeded raisins	mon, allspice, nutmeg

Mix in order given.   Pack into greased molds and
steam briskly three hours.   Fill molds only half full
to allow for swelling of the pudding.   This will keep
for days and may be reheated at will.

MARSHMALLOW PUDDING — "JUNE NIGHT"

½ pound marshmallows   ½ pint whipped cream
1 cup strong hot coffee

This is a very simple and delicious dessert.   Melt
marshmallows in a double boiler.   Add the hot
coffee; then the cream; a little vanilla flavoring if
desired.   Pour into molds and serve cold.

THANKSGIVING DAY PLUM PUDDING

1½ cups bread crumbs,
  ground
¼ cup flour
½ cup brown sugar
1 cup suet, chopped
1 cup molasses
3 eggs
½ pound seedless raisins

⅓ cup citron or candied
  orange peel
2 cups tart apples, chopped
  fine
1 cup orange juice or cider
1 teaspoon each, salt, cinnamon, clove, allspice
Grated rind 1 lemon

Cover, and let stand overnight citron, with the
fruit juice, the apples, raisins, nuts.   In the morning
add the chopped suet, sugar, bread crumbs, flour, and
seasonings.   Beat eggs well and stir in.   Turn into a
buttered mold two thirds full only.   Place mold in
a kettle of boiling water and steam all day — eight or

more hours. When reheated, return to kettle and steam another hour. Serve with Foamy or other good pudding sauce.

ORANGE PUDDING

Cover the bottom of a glass pudding dish with sliced oranges. Sprinkle over them a little sugar. Make a rich boiled custard, omitting the whites of the eggs, and pour over the oranges. Make a meringue of the stiffly beaten egg whites mixed with powdered sugar. Put on top of the custard and set into a slow oven or at 300° F. to brown lightly. Set aside to chill before using.

OLD-FASHIONED RICE PUDDING

½ cup rice	½ cup sugar
½ cup seedless raisins	¼ teaspoon salt
1 quart milk	½ teaspoon nutmeg

Wash the rice in cold water and drain. Mix it with the raisins, milk, sugar, and seasonings. Place in a buttered baking dish and bake in a slow oven until thickened — three and a half to four hours. During the first hour of cooking stir the pudding gently now and then to prevent sticking at the bottom. The dish should be quite full when set into the oven as the pudding shrinks somewhat in cooking. Serve in the same dish with cream.

RICE BAVARIAN PUDDING

1 quart milk	¼ cup sugar
¾ cup rice	1 cup grated pineapple
½ pint cream	¼ teaspoon salt

Heat the milk in double boiler.   Wash the rice and add, cooking until milk is absorbed.   Stir in the sugar and salt.   Set aside to chill.   Whip the cream and mix in.   When ready to serve pour over a cup of grated pineapple.   Serve in sherbet glasses.   The pudding may be varied by using a Maple Nut Sauce or any good crushed fruit sauce.

PRUNE WHIP, MOLDED

1 pound prunes	Juice 1 lemon
½ cup sugar	Juice 1 orange
2 tablespoons gelatine	2 egg whites

Wash prunes.   Soak overnight in water to cover. In the morning stew them until tender.   Discard the water.   Remove pits and add sugar to the prune pulp.   Dissolve gelatine in cold water.   Add to pulp with the lemon and orange juice.   Beat until foamy. Whip the egg whites until stiff and fold in.   Pour into individual molds to set.   Serve with whipped cream on top.

TUMBLE-OVER PUDDING — OLD RECIPE

This may be varied at will by using whatever fruit or berries are in season.   Make a sweetened sauce of any stewed fruit — rhubarb, apple, or berries.

Place in bottom of a buttered pudding dish. Over the rhubarb or other fruit pour a batter of any good one-egg cake. Bake in moderate oven, or at 350° F. When cooked, turn it over on a serving dish with the fruit on top. Serve with a hot lemon or nutmeg sauce.

RHUBARB BETTY

1 pound chopped rhubarb	1¾ cups coarse bread
1¼ cups sugar	crumbs
2 tablespoons butter,	1 teaspoon cinnamon
melted	¼ teaspoon salt

Mix together the rhubarb, sugar, salt, and spice. Place a layer in the buttered bottom of a pudding dish. Mix melted butter with the crumbs and sprinkle over the rhubarb. Continue until dish is full. Have buttered crumbs on top. Cover and bake forty-five minutes. Then remove cover and brown. The cooked rhubarb makes sufficient liquid. Serve with any preferred pudding sauce.

GRANDMA'S WINE JELLY

1 cup grape juice	1 tablespoon granulated gelatine
1 tablespoon lemon juice	Cold water to cover
½ cup sugar	Whites of 3 eggs

Dissolve the gelatine in cold water and place over hot water to hasten the process, stirring meanwhile.

Warm the grape-juice slightly. Dissolve the sugar in it. Add the gelatine and lemon juice. Stir all well together. Beat whites of the eggs stiff and when the jelly begins to cool and grow firm, add them to it. Make a boiled custard of the egg yolks and pour over when serving.

PUDDING SAUCES

CARAMEL SAUCE

In a freshly scoured saucepan brown three fourths cup of sugar. Lift pan from fire occasionally, so the caramel may be an even brown. When melted, pour on very slowly a cup of boiling water. Simmer until dissolved. Add half a tablespoon butter in small bits, stirring constantly to mix, and one teaspoon vanilla.

CHOCOLATE SAUCE

3 tablespoons butter	¾ cup sugar
4 tablespoons shaved chocolate	½ cup thin cream
4 tablespoons cocoa	1 teaspoon vanilla
⅛ teaspoon salt	

Melt butter in saucepan over slow fire. Add the shaved chocolate. Stir until smooth. Put in the cocoa, sugar, and cream. Stir well until dissolved. Add the salt and vanilla. Let come to boiling point and remove. Set aside to chill. Reheat when needed in double boiler.

HOT CHOCOLATE FUDGE SAUCE

2 squares grated chocolate	2 teaspoons cornstarch
1½ cups sugar	1 tablespoon butter
2 cups water	Salt, vanilla

Shave or grate the chocolate. Cook with the water and sugar until chocolate is melted. Mix cornstarch with a little cold water until dissolved and add to the mixture with the butter. Boil together three minutes, stirring constantly. Remove from fire. Add a tiny pinch of salt and the flavoring. Serve hot.

CIDER SAUCE

¾ cup sugar   2 tablespoons lemon juice
            1 full cup sweet cider

Boil all together five minutes and serve hot on holiday puddings.

CREAM PUDDING SAUCE

1 egg   1 cup cream
¾ cup powdered sugar   2 tablespoons fruit juice

Beat the egg very light. Add sugar to make a rich custard. Whip cream stiff and stir in with the fruit juice. If orange is used, grate a part of the rind for added flavor.

BOILED CUSTARD SAUCE

3 egg yolks   2 cups scalded milk
¼ cup sugar   ⅛ teaspoon salt
            1 teaspoon flavoring

Beat yolks just enough to break them up. Add sugar and salt. Mix well. Place in double boiler. Add hot milk very gradually. Stir until it thickens.

Strain. Beat up light. Flavor with vanilla, brandy, lemon juice, or any preferred flavor. This is good, hot or cold.

FOAMY SAUCE

⅓ cup butter   1 egg white
1 cup powdered sugar   2 tablespoons flavoring
               ¼ cup boiling water

Beat the butter and sugar to a cream. Add flavoring — wine, vanilla, or fruit juice — and beat again, while the bowl is set over a dish of hot water. Add the boiling water and last, the egg white beaten stiff. Beat all together until foamy.

HARD SAUCE

1½ cups powdered sugar   1 tablespoon cream
3 tablespoons butter   ¾ teaspoon vanilla

Beat butter and sugar to a cream. Add the flavoring and the cream gradually. In place of the cream one tablespoon lemon juice and half a teaspoon lemon extract may be used with a few drops of hot water.

JELLY SAUCE

½ glass currant jell   1 teaspoon cornstarch
3 tablespoons sugar   1 teaspoon butter
               ½ cup water

Any good tasty jell is suitable for this sauce. Beat it with an egg beater and mix with sugar and water.

Place over the fire to cook a few minutes, beating until it bubbles. Dissolve the cornstarch in cold water and add to the hot mixture. Cook until it thickens. Take from fire and beat in the butter.

LEMON SAUCE

1 scant cup sugar	Grated rind ½ lemon
1 level tablespoon cornstarch	2 tablespoons lemon juice
2 cups boiling water	

Dissolve the cornstarch in a little cold water. Mix with the sugar. Pour on the boiling water very slowly while stirring constantly. Add the grated rind and the butter. Boil five minutes. Remove from fire and add lemon juice.

OLD-FASHIONED NUTMEG SAUCE

1 cup sugar	2 cups boiling water
1 tablespoon flour	⅛ teaspoon salt
1 tablespoon butter	½ teaspoon grated nutmeg

Mix flour, sugar, and salt. Add boiling water while stirring to prevent lumping. Dissolve the butter in the hot mixture and boil three or four minutes. Take from the fire and add grated nutmeg. Serve hot.

MAPLE NUT SAUCE

¼ teaspoon mapleine flavoring	¼ cup broken walnut meats
1 cup maple syrup	

Add flavoring to the syrup.   Stir in the nut meats and pour over ice cream.

ORANGE SAUCE

Juice of 2 oranges	Yolks 2 eggs
1 tablespoon cornstarch	¼ cup sugar
2 tablespoons water	White of 1 egg

Dissolve cornstarch in the water.   Add orange juice and cook to thicken.   Add sugar and egg yolks slightly beaten.   Take from the fire.   Cool, and fold in the stiffly beaten egg white.   This is a good fritter sauce.

ORANGE MARMALADE SAUCE

¾ cup orange marmalade   ½ cup sugar
¼ cup water

Boil all together five minutes. Chill.   This is good over plain ice cream or with cake puddings.

QUICK PUDDING SAUCE

1 egg	3 tablespoons boiling water
1 cup sugar	1 tablespoon flavoring

Beat the egg light.   Mix with sugar.   Beat in the boiling water and cook five minutes with bowl set over hot water.   Add flavoring and serve hot.

STRAWBERRY SAUCE

1½ cups crushed strawberries   ¾ cup sugar
½ cup water

Boil sugar and water to a syrup.   When cool add the crushed strawberries.   Delicious with ice cream or sponge cake.

STRAWBERRY BUTTER

1 cup powdered sugar   ¼ cup berries, crushed
4 tablespoons butter

Cream the butter with a spoon.   Add sugar gradually.   When creamy stir in the crushed berries, beating to make a smooth mixture.   Chill until needed.   Red raspberries or peaches are also very good for fruit butters.

BUTTERSCOTCH SAUCE

1⅓ cups white sugar   1¼ cups boiling water
1 cup brown sugar   3 tablespoons butter
½ cup corn syrup (white)

Mix the sugars and the syrup.   Pour on the boiling water slowly.   Add butter and cook until a very soft ball is formed in cold water.   Serve hot.   If too thick dilute with a little milk.   Reheat over hot water.

CRANBERRIES

CRANBERRY SAUCE

1 quart cranberries   2 cups sugar
1 cup boiling water

Cover the cranberries with boiling water. When cool enough to handle, select the choice berries, which will be bright red. Put them into an agateware kettle. Pour over one cup of boiling water and cook slowly until the skins burst. Then add the sugar and cook twelve minutes more, or until the sauce has thickened.

STEWED CRANBERRIES

3 cups cranberries   1 ½ cups sugar
1 cup water

Boil sugar and water seven minutes. Add the selected berries. Cook until they burst. Strain or not, as preferred. Cool.

CRANBERRY JELLY

1 pint of cranberries   2 cups sugar, brown or white
¾ cup water

Put the washed berries in a saucepan with the water and cook until soft, covered all the time. Then rub through a sieve.   Add the sugar.   Bring to a boil and cook ten minutes.   Pour into wet molds to set.

CRANBERRY CONSERVE — "JELLY KITCHEN"

1 quart cranberries	1 full cup nut meats
1 orange	4½ cups sugar
⅓ cup seeded raisins	

Chop the cranberries fine.   Cut up the orange and use all but the bitter white skin and seeds.   Add the raisins chopped, and the chopped nut meats.   Put into a kettle with the sugar and cook very slowly to keep from burning.   Let simmer until it thickens. When done, it should have the consistency of marmalade and is very good with meat dishes, or with toast for tea.

CRANBERRY PUDDING

2 cups flour	1 teaspoon baking powder
1 cup sugar	1½ cups cranberries
1 cup milk	Butter size of a walnut, melted

Cut the berries into halves.   Remove the seeds. Sift flour and baking powder together.   Mix with other ingredients and bake in buttered pudding dish at 350° F.   Serve with a sweet sauce.

CRANBERRY MERINGUE PIE

3 cups berries	1 tablespoon butter, melted
1½ cups sugar	1 egg yolk
3 tablespoons flour	¼ teaspoon salt

Put the washed and selected berries into an enameled dish with one cup of cold water. Boil until berries burst. Then add the sugar and boil two minutes more. Mix together the flour, salt, and butter and stir in. Last, add the slightly beaten egg yolk. Mix ingredients well together. Pour into a previously baked pie crust. Cover with meringue made of two egg whites, four tablespoons sugar, one eighth teaspoon salt. Mix salt with egg whites and beat until stiff. Add sugar. Beat two minutes more. Cover pie with the meringue and brown in a slow oven — 325° F.

CRANBERRY AND PRUNE PIE

1½ cups cranberries	1 tablespoon butter
1 cup prunes	¾ cup sugar
1 tablespoon flour	

Cut berries into halves and remove seeds. Cook prunes until soft. Cut them into bits. Mix prunes and berries with flour and sugar. Turn into a pie plate with thin under crust, unbaked. Dot over with bits of butter. Place lattice strips of paste across top. Bake twenty to thirty minutes. Moderately hot oven — 375° F.

MOCK CHERRY PIE

1½ cups cranberries	¾ cup sugar
¾ cup raisins	½ cup flour
1 cup water	

Cook berries, raisins, and water together until berries are soft. Let cool. Mix sugar and flour and add to berries. Stir until sugar is dissolved. Bring to a boil and cook five minutes. Let cool a little before placing between two crusts and baking. This will make filling for two pies.

CRANBERRY TARTS — "GRANDMA'S"

1 cup cranberries, cut up	1 teaspoon butter
1 tablespoon cornstarch	2 tablespoons molasses
½ cup sugar	¼ cup boiling water

Mix cranberries with dry ingredients. Place on the fire, pouring over the boiling water. Add the molasses, butter, and a pinch of salt. Cook slowly five minutes. Cool before using.

Make small tarts from bits of paste and fill with the mixture.

PROVINCETOWN MOCK CHERRY PIE

1 cup cranberries	1 tablespoon flour
½ cup seeded raisins	2 teaspoons vanilla
1 cup sugar	½ cup boiling water

Cut the berries into halves and remove seeds. Mix with remaining dry ingredients and add the water and vanilla. Bake between two crusts in a moderate oven — 375° F.

CRANBERRY FRAPPÉ

1 quart cranberries	2 cups sugar
1 cup water	⅓ cup lemon juice

Wash and select berries. Cook with a cup of water until soft. Mash and add sugar and lemon juice. Beat well together. Strain, cool, and freeze. Very nice with game and turkey dinners.

CRANBERRY AND RAISIN TARTS

1 cup cranberries	3 tablespoons flour
½ cup seeded raisins	½ teaspoon salt
1 cup sugar	½ cup hot water

Chop together the cranberries and raisins. Mix sugar, flour, and salt, and add. Pour on a half cup boiling water and let cook in double boiler for half an hour. When cool, fill pastry shells which have been previously baked.

CRANBERRY GAME SAUCE

Make a paste of one tablespoon butter and three fourths tablespoon of flour. Pour on slowly one cup chicken or beef broth (may be made quickly with a bouillon cube), a pinch of salt, and cook until smooth and thickened. Stir in two tablespoons stewed cranberries. Cook five minutes.

CAPE COD PRESERVES AND RELISHES

CHILI SAUCE

24 ripe tomatoes
6 large onions
3 green peppers
1 quart vinegar

¾ cup sugar
2 tablespoons salt
1 tablespoon each cloves, nutmeg, powdered ginger, and allspice

Scald and peel the tomatoes. Seed the green peppers and chop with the onions, quite fine. Put all into a kettle with the vinegar and boil down until thick — a matter of two hours or so. Add the spices half an hour before taking from the fire. Seal in glass jars.

PICCALILLI — "GREENBRIAR"

½ peck green tomatoes
10 medium-sized onions
2 full cups brown sugar
3 cups vinegar

½ cup salt
2 sweet red peppers
½ cup mixed spices sewed in a bag

½ teaspoon cayenne

Slice the tomatoes; sprinkle with salt and let stand overnight. In the morning grind together the onions, red peppers, and tomatoes. Heat the vinegar and spices in a kettle; add the vegetables and boil slowly until the vinegar is nearly gone.

RHUBARB PICKLE

1 quart rhubarb, peeled
and diced
1 quart onions, chopped
1 teaspoon salt

1½ pounds brown sugar
1 teaspoon each ginger, allspice,
cloves, and cinnamon
⅛ teaspoon cayenne
1 quart vinegar

Mix ingredients and boil slowly four hours. Seal in jars.

GREEN TOMATO PRESERVE

½ peck small green tomatoes
2 tablespoons salt
1 cup vinegar
1 cup water

1 lemon, sliced thin
3 pieces ginger root
2 cups brown sugar
1 cup white sugar

Boil the tomatoes in salted water until tender, using the salt with water to cover. Drain. Boil all together the remaining ingredients until the lemon slices are clear. Add the tomatoes and cook until clear. Seal in jars for winter use.

WATERMELON PICKLE

3 quarts melon rind
1 pint vinegar

3 pounds brown sugar
1 ounce each cinnamon, clove, mace

Remove and discard the green part of the rind. Cut remaining part into small pieces. Cover with water and boil until tender. Drain. Make a syrup of remaining ingredients, tying the spices in a bag. Boil all together five minutes. Remove spice bag. Boil the syrup half an hour. Add the melon rind and simmer at back of stove two hours, when the liquid should be like a rich syrup. Seal in jars.

PRESERVED PUMPKIN

Cut a ripe pumpkin into pieces one third of an inch thick and pare them. Weigh the pieces. Take an equal weight in white sugar. Allow the juice of one lemon to each pound of pumpkin. Put the pumpkin into a bowl over night with the sugar and lemon juice. In the morning put into a kettle and cook until perfectly clear. Add the lemon peel cut into small pieces. Cook gently fifteen or twenty minutes. Remove pumpkin. Strain in a jelly bag and pour the syrup over the pumpkin. Seal while hot.

PRESERVED CUCUMBERS

When the garden has an over supply of cucumbers, they may be perfectly preserved for winter use by putting them down in the following mixture: one gallon vinegar, one cup salt, two cups brown sugar, one cup mustard.

Wash the cucumbers and put them into crocks. Cover with the mixture. The cucumbers will be crisp and fresh when taken out. Do not peel the cucumbers until wanted for use.

APRICOT MARMALADE

1 pound dried apricots 6 cups water
2 large oranges 6 cups sugar

Wash the apricots and soak overnight in one cup cold water. Reserve this water. Run the apricots through the food chopper. Peel and cut up the oranges. Put the orange pulp and one quarter of the orange peel through the chopper. Then cook together forty-five minutes slowly, the apricots, orange pulp and peel, all juices, sugar, and remaining five cups of water. Seal in jars.

ORANGE MARMALADE

3 large seedless oranges 1 lemon
4 pounds of sugar

Slice the oranges and lemon very thin. Pour over eleven tumblers of water and let stand covered for twenty-four hours. Then boil slowly for one hour. Add all the sugar and let stand another twenty-four hours. Then boil one and a half hours. Pour into jelly glasses and seal when cold.

PICKLED PEARS

8 pounds of pears 1 ounce each cinnamon bark,
4 pounds brown sugar mace, and allspice
1 quart vinegar

Steam the pears until soft. Stick a number of cloves in each pear. Boil the vinegar and spices, tied in a cheese cloth bag, together with the sugar until syrupy.

Pour over the fruit. Repeat three mornings. Seal.

CHUTNEY

1 dozen tart apples	1 tablespoon ginger
2 green peppers, seeded	1 tablespoon salt
1 onion, peeled	Juice 2 large lemons
1 cup seeded raisins	½ jar cranberry jelly
2 cups brown sugar	1 small red pepper

2 cups mild vinegar

Core and peel the apples. Chop with the peppers, raisins, and onion, or put through the meat grinder. Place in an enameled kettle with the vinegar, sugar, and jelly. Bring to a boil and let simmer one hour. Add remaining ingredients and cook very slowly another hour. Seal in sterilized jars.

SUNKISSED STRAWBERRIES

Use firm, choice strawberries. Weigh them and take an equal weight in sugar. Put into a kettle with a very little water. Bring to boiling point but do not allow to boil. Remove and spread out on a large agate pan. Cover with glass and let cook in hot sunlight until jellied. The time required depends upon the sunlight.

CANDIED ORANGE PEEL

Prepare the peel by removing as much of the loose white pulp as possible. Cut into long strips about a quarter of an inch wide, with kitchen scissors. Cover with cold water; bring to a boil and drain. Repeat this three times. Then measure the fruit and allow one cup of sugar to each cup of peel. Place in a kettle and cover with cold water. Cook slowly until the peel is clear. Remove and roll strips in sugar. Spread out to dry.

PLEASANT BAY MINCE MEAT

½ pound beef, boiled or roasted
½ pound suet, chopped
½ pound currants
½ pound seeded raisins, chopped
3 tart apples, pared and chopped

1 cup brown sugar
1 tablespoon cinnamon
⅛ cup citron, chopped
1 orange, juice and rind
1 teaspoon each salt and mace
½ teaspoon each nutmeg and cloves
1½ pints cider

Run the meat, suet, and apples through the food chopper. Place everything except the spices in a large kettle and cook until the apples are tender. Add the spices during cooking. Make at least two weeks before using. Keep covered in a crock or seal in jars.

VEGETARIAN OR GREEN TOMATO MINCE MEAT

1 peck green tomatoes
5 pounds brown sugar
1 cup vinegar
2 quarts chopped apples
2 pounds raisins, seeded and chopped
2 tablespoons each cinnamon, cloves, allspice
1 tablespoon each nutmeg and salt
½ cup lemon juice and grated rind
1 cup beef suet, chopped

Put tomatoes through a grinder. Save the juice and add to it approximately half as much water. Mix all ingredients together in a large kettle and simmer two or more hours, stirring now and then with a wooden spoon. When thickened, seal boiling hot in sterilized jars.

INDEX

INDEX

Index

Index

**A CATALOGUE OF SELECTED DOVER BOOKS
IN ALL FIELDS OF INTEREST**

A CATALOGUE OF SELECTED DOVER BOOKS
IN ALL FIELDS OF INTEREST

THE DEVIL'S DICTIONARY, Ambrose Bierce. Barbed, bitter, brilliant witticisms in the form of a dictionary. Best, most ferocious satire America has produced. 145pp. 20487-1 Pa. $1.75

ABSOLUTELY MAD INVENTIONS, A.E. Brown, H.A. Jeffcott. Hilarious, useless, or merely absurd inventions all granted patents by the U.S. Patent Office. Edible tie pin, mechanical hat tipper, etc. 57 illustrations. 125pp. 22596-8 Pa. $1.50

AMERICAN WILD FLOWERS COLORING BOOK, Paul Kennedy. Planned coverage of 48 most important wildflowers, from Rickett's collection; instructive as well as entertaining. Color versions on covers. 48pp. 8¼ x 11. 20095-7 Pa. $1.50

BIRDS OF AMERICA COLORING BOOK, John James Audubon. Rendered for coloring by Paul Kennedy. 46 of Audubon's noted illustrations: red-winged blackbird, cardinal, purple finch, towhee, etc. Original plates reproduced in full color on the covers. 48pp. 8¼ x 11. 23049-X Pa. $1.50

NORTH AMERICAN INDIAN DESIGN COLORING BOOK, Paul Kennedy. The finest examples from Indian masks, beadwork, pottery, etc. — selected and redrawn for coloring (with identifications) by well-known illustrator Paul Kennedy. 48pp. 8¼ x 11. 21125-8 Pa. $1.50

UNIFORMS OF THE AMERICAN REVOLUTION COLORING BOOK, Peter Copeland. 31 lively drawings reproduce whole panorama of military attire; each uniform has complete instructions for accurate coloring. (Not in the Pictorial Archives Series). 64pp. 8¼ x 11. 21850-3 Pa. $1.50

THE WONDERFUL WIZARD OF OZ COLORING BOOK, L. Frank Baum. Color the Yellow Brick Road and much more in 61 drawings adapted from W.W. Denslow's originals, accompanied by abridged version of text. Dorothy, Toto, Oz and the Emerald City. 61 illustrations. 64pp. 8¼ x 11. 20452-9 Pa. $1.50

CUT AND COLOR PAPER MASKS, Michael Grater. Clowns, animals, funny faces . . . simply color them in, cut them out, and put them together, and you have 9 paper masks to play with and enjoy. Complete instructions. Assembled masks shown in full color on the covers. 32pp. 8¼ x 11. 23171-2 Pa. $1.50

STAINED GLASS CHRISTMAS ORNAMENT COLORING BOOK, Carol Belanger Grafton. Brighten your Christmas season with over 100 Christmas ornaments done in a stained glass effect on translucent paper. Color them in and then hang at windows, from lights, anywhere. 32pp. 8¼ x 11. 20707-2 Pa. $1.75

CREATIVE LITHOGRAPHY AND HOW TO DO IT, Grant Arnold. Lithography as art form: working directly on stone, transfer of drawings, lithotint, mezzotint, color printing; also metal plates. Detailed, thorough. 27 illustrations. 214pp.
21208-4 Pa. $3.00

DESIGN MOTIFS OF ANCIENT MEXICO, Jorge Enciso. Vigorous, powerful ceramic stamp impressions — Maya, Aztec, Toltec, Olmec. Serpents, gods, priests, dancers, etc. 153pp. 6⅛ x 9¼.
20084-1 Pa. $2.50

AMERICAN INDIAN DESIGN AND DECORATION, Leroy Appleton. Full text, plus more than 700 precise drawings of Inca, Maya, Aztec, Pueblo, Plains, NW Coast basketry, sculpture, painting, pottery, sand paintings, metal, etc. 4 plates in color. 279pp. 8⅜ x 11¼.
22704-9 Pa. $4.50

CHINESE LATTICE DESIGNS, Daniel S. Dye. Incredibly beautiful geometric designs: circles, voluted, simple dissections, etc. Inexhaustible source of ideas, motifs. 1239 illustrations. 469pp. 6⅛ x 9¼.
23096-1 Pa. $5.00

JAPANESE DESIGN MOTIFS, Matsuya Co. Mon, or heraldic designs. Over 4000 typical, beautiful designs: birds, animals, flowers, swords, fans, geometric; all beautifully stylized. 213pp. 11⅜ x 8¼.
22874-6 Pa. $5.00

PERSPECTIVE, Jan Vredeman de Vries. 73 perspective plates from 1604 edition; buildings, townscapes, stairways, fantastic scenes. Remarkable for beauty, surrealistic atmosphere; real eye-catchers. Introduction by Adolf Placzek. 74pp. 11⅜ x 8¼.
20186-4 Pa. $2.75

EARLY AMERICAN DESIGN MOTIFS, Suzanne E. Chapman. 497 motifs, designs, from painting on wood, ceramics, appliqué, glassware, samplers, metal work, etc. Florals, landscapes, birds and animals, geometrics, letters, etc. Inexhaustible. Enlarged edition. 138pp. 8⅜ x 11¼.
22985-8 Pa. $3.50
23084-8 Clothbd. $7.95

VICTORIAN STENCILS FOR DESIGN AND DECORATION, edited by E.V. Gillon, Jr. 113 wonderful ornate Victorian pieces from German sources; florals, geometrics; borders, corner pieces; bird motifs, etc. 64pp. 9⅜ x 12¼.
21995-X Pa. $2.75

ART NOUVEAU: AN ANTHOLOGY OF DESIGN AND ILLUSTRATION FROM THE STUDIO, edited by E.V. Gillon, Jr. Graphic arts: book jackets, posters, engravings, illustrations, decorations; Crane, Beardsley, Bradley and many others. Inexhaustible. 92pp. 8⅛ x 11.
22388-4 Pa. $2.50

ORIGINAL ART DECO DESIGNS, William Rowe. First-rate, highly imaginative modern Art Deco frames, borders, compositions, alphabets, florals, insectals, Wurlitzer-types, etc. Much finest modern Art Deco. 80 plates, 8 in color. 8⅜ x 11¼.
22567-4 Pa. $3.50

HANDBOOK OF DESIGNS AND DEVICES, Clarence P. Hornung. Over 1800 basic geometric designs based on circle, triangle, square, scroll, cross, etc. Largest such collection in existence. 261pp.
20125-2 Pa. $2.75

VICTORIAN HOUSES: A TREASURY OF LESSER-KNOWN EXAMPLES, Edmund Gillon and Clay Lancaster. 116 photographs, excellent commentary illustrate distinct characteristics, many borrowings of local Victorian architecture. Octagonal houses, Americanized chalets, grand country estates, small cottages, etc. Rich heritage often overlooked. 116 plates. 11⅜ x 10. 22966-1 Pa. $4.00

STICKS AND STONES, Lewis Mumford. Great classic of American cultural history; architecture from medieval-inspired earliest forms to 20th century; evolution of structure and style, influence of environment. 21 illustrations. 113pp.
20202-X Pa. $2.50

ON THE LAWS OF JAPANESE PAINTING, Henry P. Bowie. Best substitute for training with genius Oriental master, based on years of study in Kano school. Philosophy, brushes, inks, style, etc. 66 illustrations. 117pp. 6⅛ x 9¼. 20030-2 Pa. $4.50

A HANDBOOK OF ANATOMY FOR ART STUDENTS, Arthur Thomson. Virtually exhaustive. Skeletal structure, muscles, heads, special features. Full text, anatomical figures, undraped photos. Male and female. 337 illustrations. 459pp.
21163-0 Pa. $5.00

AN ATLAS OF ANATOMY FOR ARTISTS, Fritz Schider. Finest text, working book. Full text, plus anatomical illustrations; plates by great artists showing anatomy. 593 illustrations. 192pp. 7⅞ x 10¾. 20241-0 Clothbd. $6.95

THE HUMAN FIGURE IN MOTION, Eadweard Muybridge. More than 4500 stopped-action photos, in action series, showing undraped men, women, children jumping, lying down, throwing, sitting, wrestling, carrying, etc. "Unparalleled dictionary for artists," American Artist. Taken by great 19th century photographer. 390pp. 7⅞ x 10⅝. 20204-6 Clothbd. $12.50

AN ATLAS OF ANIMAL ANATOMY FOR ARTISTS, W. Ellenberger et al. Horses, dogs, cats, lions, cattle, deer, etc. Muscles, skeleton, surface features. The basic work. Enlarged edition. 288 illustrations. 151pp. 9⅜ x 12¼. 20082-5 Pa. $4.50

LETTER FORMS: 110 COMPLETE ALPHABETS, Frederick Lambert. 110 sets of capital letters; 16 lower case alphabets; 70 sets of numbers and other symbols. Edited and expanded by Theodore Menten. 110pp. 8⅛ x 11. 22872-X Pa. $3.00

THE METHODS OF CONSTRUCTION OF CELTIC ART, George Bain. Simple geometric techniques for making wonderful Celtic interlacements, spirals, Kells-type initials, animals, humans, etc. Unique for artists, craftsmen. Over 500 illustrations. 160pp. 9 x 12. USO 22923-8 Pa. $4.00

SCULPTURE, PRINCIPLES AND PRACTICE, Louis Slobodkin. Step by step approach to clay, plaster, metals, stone; classical and modern. 253 drawings, photos. 255pp. 8⅛ x 11. 22960-2 Pa. $5.00

THE ART OF ETCHING, E.S. Lumsden. Clear, detailed instructions for etching, drypoint, softground, aquatint; from 1st sketch to print. Very detailed, thorough. 200 illustrations. 376pp. 20049-3 Pa. $3.75

CONSTRUCTION OF AMERICAN FURNITURE TREASURES, Lester Margon. 344 detail drawings, complete text on constructing exact reproductions of 38 early American masterpieces: Hepplewhite sideboard, Duncan Phyfe drop-leaf table, mantel clock, gate-leg dining table, Pa. German cupboard, more. 38 plates. 54 photographs. 168pp. 8⅜ x 11¼.   23056-2 Pa. $4.00

JEWELRY MAKING AND DESIGN, Augustus F. Rose, Antonio Cirino. Professional secrets revealed in thorough, practical guide: tools, materials, processes; rings, brooches, chains, cast pieces, enamelling, setting stones, etc. Do not confuse with skimpy introductions: beginner can use, professional can learn from it. Over 200 illustrations. 306pp.   21750-7 Pa. $3.00

METALWORK AND ENAMELLING, Herbert Maryon. Generally coneeded best all-around book. Countless trade secrets: materials, tools, soldering, filigree, setting, inlay, niello, repoussé, casting, polishing, etc. For beginner or expert. Author was foremost British expert. 330 illustrations. 335pp.   22702-2 Pa. $3.50

WEAVING WITH FOOT-POWER LOOMS, Edward F. Worst. Setting up a loom, beginning to weave, constructing equipment, using dyes, more, plus over 285 drafts of traditional patterns including Colonial and Swedish weaves. More than 200 other figures. For beginning and advanced. 275pp. 8¾ x 6⅜.   23064-3 Pa. $4.50

WEAVING A NAVAJO BLANKET, Gladys A. Reichard. Foremost anthropologist studied under Navajo women, reveals every step in process from wool, dyeing, spinning, setting up loom, designing, weaving. Much history, symbolism. With this book you could make one yourself. 97 illustrations. 222pp.   22992-0 Pa. $3.00

NATURAL DYES AND HOME DYEING, Rita J. Adrosko. Use natural ingredients: bark, flowers, leaves, lichens, insects etc. Over 135 specific recipes from historical sources for cotton, wool, other fabrics. Genuine premodern handicrafts. 12 illustrations. 160pp.   22688-3 Pa. $2.00

THE HAND DECORATION OF FABRICS, Francis J. Kafka. Outstanding, profusely illustrated guide to stenciling, batik, block printing, tie dyeing, freehand painting, silk screen printing, and novelty decoration. 356 illustrations. 198pp. 6 x 9.
                                                   21401-X Pa. $3.00

THOMAS NAST: CARTOONS AND ILLUSTRATIONS, with text by Thomas Nast St. Hill. Father of American political cartooning. Cartoons that destroyed Tweed Ring; inflation, free love, church and state; original Republican elephant and Democratic donkey; Santa Claus; more. 117 illustrations. 146pp. 9 x 12.
                                                   22983-1 Pa. $4.00
                                                   23067-8 Clothbd. $8.50

FREDERIC REMINGTON: 173 DRAWINGS AND ILLUSTRATIONS. Most famous of the Western artists, most responsible for our myths about the American West in its untamed days. Complete reprinting of *Drawings of Frederic Remington* (1897), plus other selections. 4 additional drawings in color on covers. 140pp. 9 x 12.
                                                   20714-5 Pa. $3.95

EARLY NEW ENGLAND GRAVESTONE RUBBINGS, Edmund V. Gillon, Jr. 43 photographs, 226 rubbings show heavily symbolic, macabre, sometimes humorous primitive American art. Up to early 19th century. 207pp. 8⅜ x 11¼.
21380-3 Pa. $4.00

L.J.M. DAGUERRE: THE HISTORY OF THE DIORAMA AND THE DAGUERREOTYPE, Helmut and Alison Gernsheim. Definitive account. Early history, life and work of Daguerre; discovery of daguerreotype process; diffusion abroad; other early photography. 124 illustrations. 226pp. 6⅙ x 9¼. 22290-X Pa. $4.00

PHOTOGRAPHY AND THE AMERICAN SCENE, Robert Taft. The basic book on American photography as art, recording form, 1839-1889. Development, influence on society, great photographers, types (portraits, war, frontier, etc.), whatever else needed. Inexhaustible. Illustrated with 322 early photos, daguerreotypes, tintypes, stereo slides, etc. 546pp. 6⅛ x 9¼. 21201-7 Pa. $5.95

PHOTOGRAPHIC SKETCHBOOK OF THE CIVIL WAR, Alexander Gardner. Reproduction of 1866 volume with 100 on-the-field photographs: Manassas, Lincoln on battlefield, slave pens, etc. Introduction by E.F. Bleiler. 224pp. 10¾ x 9.
22731-6 Pa. $5.00

THE MOVIES: A PICTURE QUIZ BOOK, Stanley Appelbaum & Hayward Cirker. Match stars with their movies, name actors and actresses, test your movie skill with 241 stills from 236 great movies, 1902-1959. Indexes of performers and films. 128pp. 8⅜ x 9¼. 20222-4 Pa. $2.50

THE TALKIES, Richard Griffith. Anthology of features, articles from Photoplay, 1928-1940, reproduced complete. Stars, famous movies, technical features, fabulous ads, etc.; Garbo, Chaplin, King Kong, Lubitsch, etc. 4 color plates, scores of illustrations. 327pp. 8⅜ x 11¼. 22762-6 Pa. $6.95

THE MOVIE MUSICAL FROM VITAPHONE TO "42ND STREET," edited by Miles Kreuger. Relive the rise of the movie musical as reported in the pages of Photoplay magazine (1926-1933): every movie review, cast list, ad, and record review; every significant feature article, production still, biography, forecast, and gossip story. Profusely illustrated. 367pp. 8⅜ x 11¼. 23154-2 Pa. $7.95

JOHANN SEBASTIAN BACH, Philipp Spitta. Great classic of biography, musical commentary, with hundreds of pieces analyzed. Also good for Bach's contemporaries. 450 musical examples. Total of 1799pp.
EUK 22278-0, 22279-9 Clothbd., Two vol. set $25.00

BEETHOVEN AND HIS NINE SYMPHONIES, Sir George Grove. Thorough history, analysis, commentary on symphonies and some related pieces. For either beginner or advanced student. 436 musical passages. 407pp. 20334-4 Pa. $4.00

MOZART AND HIS PIANO CONCERTOS, Cuthbert Girdlestone. The only full-length study. Detailed analyses of all 21 concertos, sources; 417 musical examples. 509pp. 21271-8 Pa. $6.00

THE FITZWILLIAM VIRGINAL BOOK, edited by J. Fuller Maitland, W.B. Squire. Famous early 17th century collection of keyboard music, 300 works by Morley, Byrd, Bull, Gibbons, etc. Modern notation. Total of 938pp. 8⅜ x 11.
ECE 21068-5, 21069-3 Pa., Two vol. set $15.00

COMPLETE STRING QUARTETS, Wolfgang A. Mozart. Breitkopf and Härtel edition. All 23 string quartets plus alternate slow movement to K156. Study score. 277pp. 9⅜ x 12¼.
22372-8 Pa. $6.00

COMPLETE SONG CYCLES, Franz Schubert. Complete piano, vocal music of Die Schöne Müllerin, Die Winterreise, Schwanengesang. Also Drinker English singing translations. Breitkopf and Härtel edition. 217pp. 9⅜ x 12¼.
22649-2 Pa. $4.50

THE COMPLETE PRELUDES AND ETUDES FOR PIANOFORTE SOLO, Alexander Scriabin. All the preludes and etudes including many perfectly spun miniatures. Edited by K.N. Igumnov and Y.I. Mil'shteyn. 250pp. 9 x 12.
22919-X Pa. $5.00

TRISTAN UND ISOLDE, Richard Wagner. Full orchestral score with complete instrumentation. Do not confuse with piano reduction. Commentary by Felix Mottl, great Wagnerian conductor and scholar. Study score. 655pp. 8⅛ x 11.
22915-7 Pa. $11.95

FAVORITE SONGS OF THE NINETIES, ed. Robert Fremont. Full reproduction, including covers, of 88 favorites: Ta-Ra-Ra-Boom-De-Aye, The Band Played On, Bird in a Gilded Cage, Under the Bamboo Tree, After the Ball, etc. 401pp. 9 x 12.
EBE 21536-9 Pa. $6.95

SOUSA'S GREAT MARCHES IN PIANO TRANSCRIPTION: ORIGINAL SHEET MUSIC OF 23 WORKS, John Philip Sousa. Selected by Lester S. Levy. Playing edition includes: The Stars and Stripes Forever, The Thunderer, The Gladiator, King Cotton, Washington Post, much more. 24 illustrations. 111pp. 9 x 12.
USO 23132-1 Pa. $3.50

CLASSIC PIANO RAGS, selected with an introduction by Rudi Blesh. Best ragtime music (1897-1922) by Scott Joplin, James Scott, Joseph F. Lamb, Tom Turpin, 9 others. Printed from best original sheet music, plus covers. 364pp. 9 x 12.
EBE 20469-3 Pa. $6.95

ANALYSIS OF CHINESE CHARACTERS, C.D. Wilder, J.H. Ingram. 1000 most important characters analyzed according to primitives, phonetics, historical development. Traditional method offers mnemonic aid to beginner, intermediate student of Chinese, Japanese. 365pp.
23045-7 Pa. $4.00

MODERN CHINESE: A BASIC COURSE, Faculty of Peking University. Self study, classroom course in modern Mandarin. Records contain phonetics, vocabulary, sentences, lessons. 249 page book contains all recorded text, translations, grammar, vocabulary, exercises. Best course on market. 3 12" 33⅓ monaural records, book, album.
98832-5 Set $12.50

THE BEST DR. THORNDYKE DETECTIVE STORIES, R. Austin Freeman. The Case of Oscar Brodski, The Moabite Cipher, and 5 other favorites featuring the great scientific detective, plus his long-believed-lost first adventure — 31 New Inn — reprinted here for the first time. Edited by E.F. Bleiler. USO 20388-3 Pa. $3.00

BEST "THINKING MACHINE" DETECTIVE STORIES, Jacques Futrelle. The Problem of Cell 13 and 11 other stories about Prof. Augustus S.F.X. Van Dusen, including two "lost" stories. First reprinting of several. Edited by E.F. Bleiler. 241pp. 20537-1 Pa. $3.00

UNCLE SILAS, J. Sheridan LeFanu. Victorian Gothic mystery novel, considered by many best of period, even better than Collins or Dickens. Wonderful psychological terror. Introduction by Frederick Shroyer. 436pp. 21715-9 Pa. $4.00

BEST DR. POGGIOLI DETECTIVE STORIES, T.S. Stribling. 15 best stories from EQMM and The Saint offer new adventures in Mexico, Florida, Tennessee hills as Poggioli unravels mysteries and combats Count Jalacki. 217pp. 23227-1 Pa. $3.00

EIGHT DIME NOVELS, selected with an introduction by E.F. Bleiler. Adventures of Old King Brady, Frank James, Nick Carter, Deadwood Dick, Buffalo Bill, The Steam Man, Frank Merriwell, and Horatio Alger — 1877 to 1905. Important, entertaining popular literature in facsimile reprint, with original covers. 190pp. 9 x 12. 22975-0 Pa. $3.50

ALICE'S ADVENTURES UNDER GROUND, Lewis Carroll. Facsimile of ms. Carroll gave Alice Liddell in 1864. Different in many ways from final Alice. Handlettered, illustrated by Carroll. Introduction by Martin Gardner. 128pp. 21482-6 Pa. $1.50

ALICE IN WONDERLAND COLORING BOOK, Lewis Carroll. Pictures by John Tenniel. Large-size versions of the famous illustrations of Alice, Cheshire Cat, Mad Hatter and all the others, waiting for your crayons. Abridged text. 36 illustrations. 64pp. 8¼ x 11. 22853-3 Pa. $1.50

AVENTURES D'ALICE AU PAYS DES MERVEILLES, Lewis Carroll. Bué's translation of "Alice" into French, supervised by Carroll himself. Novel way to learn language. (No English text.) 42 Tenniel illustrations. 196pp. 22836-3 Pa. $2.50

MYTHS AND FOLK TALES OF IRELAND, Jeremiah Curtin. 11 stories that are Irish versions of European fairy tales and 9 stories from the Fenian cycle — 20 tales of legend and magic that comprise an essential work in the history of folklore. 256pp. 22430-9 Pa. $3.00

EAST O' THE SUN AND WEST O' THE MOON, George W. Dasent. Only full edition of favorite, wonderful Norwegian fairytales — Why the Sea is Salt, Boots and the Troll, etc. — with 77 illustrations by Kittelsen & Werenskiöld. 418pp. 22521-6 Pa. $4.00

PERRAULT'S FAIRY TALES, Charles Perrault and Gustave Doré. Original versions of Cinderella, Sleeping Beauty, Little Red Riding Hood, etc. in best translation, with 34 wonderful illustrations by Gustave Doré. 117pp. 8⅛ x 11. 22311-6 Pa. $2.50

MOTHER GOOSE'S MELODIES. Facsimile of fabulously rare Munroe and Francis "copyright 1833" Boston edition. Familiar and unusual rhymes, wonderful old woodcut illustrations. Edited by E.F. Bleiler. 128pp. 4½ x 6⅜. 22577-1 Pa. $1.50

MOTHER GOOSE IN HIEROGLYPHICS. Favorite nursery rhymes presented in rebus form for children. Fascinating 1849 edition reproduced in toto, with key. Introduction by E.F. Bleiler. About 400 woodcuts. 64pp. 6⅞ x 5¼. 20745-5 Pa. $1.00

PETER PIPER'S PRACTICAL PRINCIPLES OF PLAIN & PERFECT PRONUNCIATION. Alliterative jingles and tongue-twisters. Reproduction in full of 1830 first American edition. 25 spirited woodcuts. 32pp. 4½ x 6⅜. 22560-7 Pa. $1.00

MARMADUKE MULTIPLY'S MERRY METHOD OF MAKING MINOR MATHEMATICIANS. Fellow to Peter Piper, it teaches multiplication table by catchy rhymes and woodcuts. 1841 Munroe & Francis edition. Edited by E.F. Bleiler. 103pp. 4⅝ x 6.
22773-1 Pa. $1.25
20171-6 Clothbd. $3.00

THE NIGHT BEFORE CHRISTMAS, Clement Moore. Full text, and woodcuts from original 1848 book. Also critical, historical material. 19 illustrations. 40pp. 4⅝ x 6. 22797-9 Pa. $1.25

THE KING OF THE GOLDEN RIVER, John Ruskin. Victorian children's classic of three brothers, their attempts to reach the Golden River, what becomes of them. Facsimile of original 1889 edition. 22 illustrations. 56pp. 4⅝ x 6⅜.
20066-3 Pa. $1.50

DREAMS OF THE RAREBIT FIEND, Winsor McCay. Pioneer cartoon strip, unexcelled for beauty, imagination, in 60 full sequences. Incredible technical virtuosity, wonderful visual wit. Historical introduction. 62pp. 8⅜ x 11¼. 21347-1 Pa. $2.50

THE KATZENJAMMER KIDS, Rudolf Dirks. In full color, 14 strips from 1906-7; full of imagination, characteristic humor. Classic of great historical importance. Introduction by August Derleth. 32pp. 9¼ x 12¼. 23005-8 Pa. $2.00

LITTLE ORPHAN ANNIE AND LITTLE ORPHAN ANNIE IN COSMIC CITY, Harold Gray. Two great sequences from the early strips: our curly-haired heroine defends the Warbucks' financial empire and, then, takes on meanie Phineas P. Pinchpenny. Leapin' lizards! 178pp. 6⅛ x 8⅜. 23107-0 Pa. $2.00

THE BEST OF GLUYAS WILLIAMS. 100 drawings by one of America's finest cartoonists: The Day a Cake of Ivory Soap Sank at Proctor & Gamble's, At the Life Insurance Agents' Banquet, and many other gems from the 20's and 30's. 118pp. 8⅜ x 11¼. 22737-5 Pa. $2.50

THE MAGIC MOVING PICTURE BOOK, Bliss, Sands & Co. The pictures in this book move! Volcanoes erupt, a house burns, a serpentine dancer wiggles her way through a number. By using a specially ruled acetate screen provided, you can obtain these and 15 other startling effects. Originally "The Motograph Moving Picture Book." 32pp. 8¼ x 11. 23224-7 Pa. $1.75

STRING FIGURES AND HOW TO MAKE THEM, Caroline F. Jayne. Fullest, clearest instructions on string figures from around world: Eskimo, Navajo, Lapp, Europe, more. Cats cradle, moving spear, lightning, stars. Introduction by A.C. Haddon. 950 illustrations. 407pp. 20152-X Pa. $3.50

PAPER FOLDING FOR BEGINNERS, William D. Murray and Francis J. Rigney. Clearest book on market for making origami sail boats, roosters, frogs that move legs, cups, bonbon boxes. 40 projects. More than 275 illustrations. Photographs. 94pp. 20713-7 Pa. $1.25

INDIAN SIGN LANGUAGE, William Tomkins. Over 525 signs developed by Sioux, Blackfoot, Cheyenne, Arapahoe and other tribes. Written instructions and diagrams: how to make words, construct sentences. Also 290 pictographs of Sioux and Ojibway tribes. 111pp. 6⅛ x 9¼. 22029-X Pa. $1.50

BOOMERANGS: HOW TO MAKE AND THROW THEM, Bernard S. Mason. Easy to make and throw, dozens of designs: cross-stick, pinwheel, boomabird, tumblestick, Australian curved stick boomerang. Complete throwing instructions. All safe. 99pp. 23028-7 Pa. $1.75

25 KITES THAT FLY, Leslie Hunt. Full, easy to follow instructions for kites made from inexpensive materials. Many novelties. Reeling, raising, designing your own. 70 illustrations. 110pp. 22550-X Pa. $1.25

TRICKS AND GAMES ON THE POOL TABLE, Fred Herrmann. 79 tricks and games, some solitaires, some for 2 or more players, some competitive; mystifying shots and throws, unusual carom, tricks involving cork, coins, a hat, more. 77 figures. 95pp. 21814-7 Pa. $1.25

WOODCRAFT AND CAMPING, Bernard S. Mason. How to make a quick emergency shelter, select woods that will burn immediately, make do with limited supplies, etc. Also making many things out of wood, rawhide, bark, at camp. Formerly titled Woodcraft. 295 illustrations. 580pp. 21951-8 Pa. $4.00

AN INTRODUCTION TO CHESS MOVES AND TACTICS SIMPLY EXPLAINED, Leonard Barden. Informal intermediate introduction: reasons for moves, tactics, openings, traps, positional play, endgame. Isolates patterns. 102pp. USO 21210-6 Pa. $1.35

LASKER'S MANUAL OF CHESS, Dr. Emanuel Lasker. Great world champion offers very thorough coverage of all aspects of chess. Combinations, position play, openings, endgame, aesthetics of chess, philosophy of struggle, much more. Filled with analyzed games. 390pp. 20640-8 Pa. $4.00

DRIED FLOWERS, Sarah Whitlock and Martha Rankin. Concise, clear, practical guide to dehydration, glycerinizing, pressing plant material, and more. Covers use of silica gel. 12 drawings. Originally titled "New Techniques with Dried Flowers." 32pp. 21802-3 Pa. $1.00

ABC OF POULTRY RAISING, J.H. Florea. Poultry expert, editor tells how to raise chickens on home or small business basis. Breeds, feeding, housing, laying, etc. Very concrete, practical. 50 illustrations. 256pp. 23201-8 Pa. $3.00

HOW INDIANS USE WILD PLANTS FOR FOOD, MEDICINE & CRAFTS, Frances Densmore. Smithsonian, Bureau of American Ethnology report presents wealth of material on nearly 200 plants used by Chippewas of Minnesota and Wisconsin. 33 plates plus 122pp. of text. 6⅛ x 9¼. 23019-8 Pa. $2.50

THE HERBAL OR GENERAL HISTORY OF PLANTS, John Gerard. The 1633 edition revised and enlarged by Thomas Johnson. Containing almost 2850 plant descriptions and 2705 superb illustrations, Gerard's Herbal is a monumental work, the book all modern English herbals are derived from, and the one herbal every serious enthusiast should have in its entirety. Original editions are worth perhaps $750. 1678pp. 8½ x 12¼. 23147-X Clothbd. $50.00

A MODERN HERBAL, Margaret Grieve. Much the fullest, most exact, most useful compilation of herbal material. Gigantic alphabetical encyclopedia, from aconite to zedoary, gives botanical information, medical properties, folklore, economic uses, and much else. Indispensable to serious reader. 161 illustrations. 888pp. 6½ x 9¼. USO 22798-7, 22799-5 Pa., Two vol. set $10.00

HOW TO KNOW THE FERNS, Frances T. Parsons. Delightful classic. Identification, fern lore, for Eastern and Central U.S.A. Has introduced thousands to interesting life form. 99 illustrations. 215pp. 20740-4 Pa. $2.75

THE MUSHROOM HANDBOOK, Louis C.C. Krieger. Still the best popular handbook. Full descriptions of 259 species, extremely thorough text, habitats, luminescence, poisons, folklore, etc. 32 color plates; 126 other illustrations. 560pp. 21861-9 Pa. $4.50

HOW TO KNOW THE WILD FRUITS, Maude G. Peterson. Classic guide covers nearly 200 trees, shrubs, smaller plants of the U.S. arranged by color of fruit and then by family. Full text provides names, descriptions, edibility, uses. 80 illustrations. 400pp. 22943-2 Pa. $4.00

COMMON WEEDS OF THE UNITED STATES, U.S. Department of Agriculture. Covers 220 important weeds with illustration, maps, botanical information, plant lore for each. Over 225 illustrations. 463pp. 6⅛ x 9¼. 20504-5 Pa. $4.50

HOW TO KNOW THE WILD FLOWERS, Mrs. William S. Dana. Still best popular book for East and Central USA. Over 500 plants easily identified, with plant lore; arranged according to color and flowering time. 174 plates. 459pp. 20332-8 Pa. $3.50

CATALOGUE OF DOVER BOOKS

DRIED FLOWERS, Sarah Whitlock and Martha Rankin. Concise, clear, practical guide to dehydration, glycerinizing, pressing plant material, and more. Covers use of silica gel. 12 drawings. Originally titled "New Techniques with Dried Flowers." 32pp. 21802-3 Pa. $1.00

ABC OF POULTRY RAISING, J.H. Florea. Poultry expert, editor tells how to raise chickens on home or small business basis. Breeds, feeding, housing, laying, etc. Very concrete, practical. 50 illustrations. 256pp. 23201-8 Pa. $3.00

HOW INDIANS USE WILD PLANTS FOR FOOD, MEDICINE & CRAFTS, Frances Densmore. Smithsonian, Bureau of American Ethnology report presents wealth of material on nearly 200 plants used by Chippewas of Minnesota and Wisconsin. 33 plates plus 122pp. of text. 6⅛ x 9¼. 23019-8 Pa. $2.50

THE HERBAL OR GENERAL HISTORY OF PLANTS, John Gerard. The 1633 edition revised and enlarged by Thomas Johnson. Containing almost 2850 plant descriptions and 2705 superb illustrations, Gerard's Herbal is a monumental work, the book all modern English herbals are derived from, and the one herbal every serious enthusiast should have in its entirety. Original editions are worth perhaps $750. 1678pp. 8½ x 12¼. 23147-X Clothbd. $50.00

A MODERN HERBAL, Margaret Grieve. Much the fullest, most exact, most useful compilation of herbal material. Gigantic alphabetical encyclopedia, from aconite to zedoary, gives botanical information, medical properties, folklore, economic uses, and much else. Indispensable to serious reader. 161 illustrations. 888pp. 6½ x 9¼. USO 22798-7, 22799-5 Pa., Two vol. set $10.00

HOW TO KNOW THE FERNS, Frances T. Parsons. Delightful classic. Identification, fern lore, for Eastern and Central U.S.A. Has introduced thousands to interesting life form. 99 illustrations. 215pp. 20740-4 Pa. $2.75

THE MUSHROOM HANDBOOK, Louis C.C. Krieger. Still the best popular handbook. Full descriptions of 259 species, extremely thorough text, habitats, luminescence, poisons, folklore, etc. 32 color plates; 126 other illustrations. 560pp. 21861-9 Pa. $4.50

HOW TO KNOW THE WILD FRUITS, Maude G. Peterson. Classic guide covers nearly 200 trees, shrubs, smaller plants of the U.S. arranged by color of fruit and then by family. Full text provides names, descriptions, edibility, uses. 80 illustrations. 400pp. 22943-2 Pa. $4.00

COMMON WEEDS OF THE UNITED STATES, U.S. Department of Agriculture. Covers 220 important weeds with illustration, maps, botanical information, plant lore for each. Over 225 illustrations. 463pp. 6⅛ x 9¼. 20504-5 Pa. $4.50

HOW TO KNOW THE WILD FLOWERS, Mrs. William S. Dana. Still best popular book for East and Central USA. Over 500 plants easily identified, with plant lore; arranged according to color and flowering time. 174 plates. 459pp. 20332-8 Pa. $3.50

THE STYLE OF PALESTRINA AND THE DISSONANCE, Knud Jeppesen. Standard analysis of rhythm, line, harmony, accented and unaccented dissonances. Also pre-Palestrina dissonances. 306pp. 22386-8 Pa. $4.50

DOVER OPERA GUIDE AND LIBRETTO SERIES prepared by Ellen H. Bleiler. Each volume contains everything needed for background, complete enjoyment: complete libretto, new English translation with all repeats, biography of composer and librettist, early performance history, musical lore, much else. All volumes lavishly illustrated with performance photos, portraits, similar material. Do not confuse with skimpy performance booklets.

CARMEN, Georges Bizet. 66 illustrations. 222pp. 22111-3 Pa. $3.00
DON GIOVANNI, Wolfgang A. Mozart. 92 illustrations. 209pp. 21134-7 Pa. $2.50
LA BOHÈME, Giacomo Puccini. 73 illustrations. 124pp. USO 20404-9 Pa. $1.75
ÄIDA, Giuseppe Verdi. 76 illustrations. 181pp. 20405-7 Pa. $2.25
LUCIA DI LAMMERMOOR, Gaetano Donizetti. 44 illustrations. 186pp.
22110-5 Pa. $2.00

ANTONIO STRADIVARI: HIS LIFE AND WORK, W. H. Hill, et al. Great work of musicology. Construction methods, woods, varnishes, known instruments, types of instruments, life, special features. Introduction by Sydney Beck. 98 illustrations, plus 4 color plates. 315pp. 20425-1 Pa. $4.00

MUSIC FOR THE PIANO, James Friskin, Irwin Freundlich. Both famous, little-known compositions; 1500 to 1950's. Listing, description, classification, technical aspects for student, teacher, performer. Indispensable for enlarging repertory. 448pp.
22918-1 Pa. $4.00

PIANOS AND THEIR MAKERS, Alfred Dolge. Leading inventor offers full history of piano technology, earliest models to 1910. Types, makers, components, mechanisms, musical aspects. Very strong on offtrail models, inventions; also player pianos. 300 illustrations. 581pp. 22856-8 Pa. $5.00

KEYBOARD MUSIC, J.S. Bach. Bach-Gesellschaft edition. For harpsichord, piano, other keyboard instruments. English Suites, French Suites, Six Partitas, Goldberg Variations, Two-Part Inventions, Three-Part Sinfonias. 312pp. 8⅛ x 11.
22360-4 Pa. $5.00

COMPLETE STRING QUARTETS, Ludwig van Beethoven. Breitkopf and Härtel edition. 6 quartets of Opus 18; 3 quartets of Opus 59; Opera 74, 95, 127, 130, 131, 132, 135 and Grosse Fuge. Study score. 434pp. 9⅜ x 12¼. 22361-2 Pa. $7.95

COMPLETE PIANO SONATAS AND VARIATIONS FOR SOLO PIANO, Johannes Brahms. All sonatas, five variations on themes from Schumann, Paganini, Handel, etc. Vienna Gesellschaft der Musikfreunde edition. 178pp. 9 x 12. 22650-6 Pa. $4.50

PIANO MUSIC 1888-1905, Claude Debussy. Deux Arabesques, Suite Bergamesque, Masques, 1st series of Images, etc. 9 others, in corrected editions. 175pp. 9⅜ x 12¼. 22771-5 Pa. $4.00

INCIDENTS OF TRAVEL IN YUCATAN, John L. Stephens. Classic (1843) exploration of jungles of Yucatan, looking for evidences of Maya civilization. Travel adventures, Mexican and Indian culture, etc. Total of 669pp.
20926-1, 20927-X Pa., Two vol. set $6.00

LIVING MY LIFE, Emma Goldman. Candid, no holds barred account by foremost American anarchist: her own life, anarchist movement, famous contemporaries, ideas and their impact. Struggles and confrontations in America, plus deportation to U.S.S.R. Shocking inside account of persecution of anarchists under Lenin. 13 plates. Total of 944pp. 22543-7, 22544-5 Pa., Two vol. set $9.00

AMERICAN INDIANS, George Catlin. Classic account of life among Plains Indians: ceremonies, hunt, warfare, etc. Dover edition reproduces for first time all original paintings. 312 plates. 572pp. of text. 6⅛ x 9¼.
22118-0, 22119-9 Pa., Two vol. set $8.00
22140-7, 22144-X Clothbd., Two vol. set $16.00.

THE INDIANS' BOOK, Natalie Curtis. Lore, music, narratives, drawings by Indians, collected from cultures of U.S.A. 149 songs in full notation. 45 illustrations. 583pp. 6⅝ x 9⅜. 21939-9 Pa. $6.95

INDIAN BLANKETS AND THEIR MAKERS, George Wharton James. History, old style wool blankets, changes brought about by traders, symbolism of design and color, a Navajo weaver at work, outline blanket, Kachina blankets, more. Emphasis on Navajo. 130 illustrations, 32 in color. 230pp. 6⅛ x 9¼. 22996-3 Pa. $5.00
23068-6 Clothbd. $10.00

AN INTRODUCTION TO THE STUDY OF THE MAYA HIEROGLYPHS, Sylvanus Griswold Morley. Classic study by one of the truly great figures in hieroglyph research. Still the best introduction for the student for reading Maya hieroglyphs. New introduction by J. Eric S. Thompson. 117 illustrations. 284pp. 23108-9 Pa. $4.00

THE ANALECTS OF CONFUCIUS, THE GREAT LEARNING, DOCTRINE OF THE MEAN, Confucius. Edited by James Legge. Full Chinese text, standard English translation on same page, Chinese commentators, editor's annotations; dictionary of characters at rear, plus grammatical comment. Finest edition anywhere of one of world's greatest thinkers. 503pp. 22746-4 Pa. $5.00

THE I CHING (THE BOOK OF CHANGES), translated by James Legge. Complete translation of basic text plus appendices by Confucius, and Chinese commentary of most penetrating divination manual ever prepared. Indispensable to study of early Oriental civilizations, to modern inquiring reader. 448pp.
21062-6 Pa. $3.50

THE EGYPTIAN BOOK OF THE DEAD, E.A. Wallis Budge. Complete reproduction of Ani's papyrus, finest ever found. Full hieroglyphic text, interlinear transliteration, word for word translation, smooth translation. Basic work, for Egyptology, for modern study of psychic matters. Total of 533pp. 6½ x 9¼.
EBE 21866-X Pa. $4.95

CATALOGUE OF DOVER BOOKS

BUILD YOUR OWN LOW-COST HOME, L.O. Anderson, H.F. Zornig. U.S. Dept. of Agriculture sets of plans, full, detailed, for 11 houses: A-Frame, circular, conventional. Also construction manual. Save hundreds of dollars. 204pp. 11 x 16.
21525-3 Pa. $6.00

HOW TO BUILD A WOOD-FRAME HOUSE, L.O. Anderson. Comprehensive, easy to follow U.S. Government manual: placement, foundations, framing, sheathing, roof, insulation, plaster, finishing — almost everything else. 179 illustrations. 223pp. 7⅞ x 10¾.
22954-8 Pa. $3.50

CONCRETE, MASONRY AND BRICKWORK, U.S. Department of the Army. Practical handbook for the home owner and small builder manual contains basic principles, techniques, and important background information on construction with concrete, concrete blocks, and brick. 177 figures, 37 tables. 200pp. 6½ x 9¼.
23203-4 Pa. $4.00

THE STANDARD BOOK OF QUILT MAKING AND COLLECTING, Marguerite Ickis. Full information, full-sized patterns for making 46 traditional quilts, also 150 other patterns. Quilted cloths, lamé, satin quilts, etc. 483 illustrations. 273pp. 6⅞ x 9⅝.
20582-7 Pa. $3.50

101 PATCHWORK PATTERNS, Ruby S. McKim. 101 beautiful, immediately useable patterns, full-size, modern and traditional. Also general information, estimating, quilt lore. 124pp. 7⅞ x 10¾.
20773-0 Pa. $2.50

KNIT YOUR OWN NORWEGIAN SWEATERS, Dale Yarn Company. Complete instructions for 50 authentic sweaters, hats, mittens, gloves, caps, etc. Thoroughly modern designs that command high prices in stores. 24 patterns, 24 color photographs. Nearly 100 charts and other illustrations. 58pp. 8⅜ x 11¼.
23031-7 Pa. $2.50

IRON-ON TRANSFER PATTERNS FOR CREWEL AND EMBROIDERY FROM EARLY AMERICAN SOURCES, edited by Rita Weiss. 75 designs, borders, alphabets, from traditional American sources printed on translucent paper in transfer ink. Reuseable. Instructions. Test patterns. 24pp. 8¼ x 11.
23162-3 Pa. $1.50

AMERICAN INDIAN NEEDLEPOINT DESIGNS FOR PILLOWS, BELTS, HANDBAGS AND OTHER PROJECTS, Roslyn Epstein. 37 authentic American Indian designs adapted for modern needlepoint projects. Grid backing makes designs easily transferable to canvas. 48pp. 8¼ x 11.
22973-4 Pa. $1.50

CHARTED FOLK DESIGNS FOR CROSS-STITCH EMBROIDERY, Maria Foris & Andreas Foris. 278 charted folk designs, most in 2 colors, from Danube region: florals, fantastic beasts, geometrics, traditional symbols, more. Border and central patterns. 77pp. 8¼ x 11.
USO 23191-7 Pa. $2.00

Prices subject to change without notice.
Available at your book dealer or write for free catalogue to Dept. GI, Dover Publications, Inc., 180 Varick St., N.Y., N.Y. 10014. Dover publishes more than 150 books each year on science, elementary and advanced mathematics, biology, music, art, literary history, social sciences and other areas.